#insidejob

Discover. Imagine. Achieve.

MARK SEPHTON

ISBN: 1502972085
ISBN – 13: 978-1502972088

Edited by Meredith Pruden
Cover and Layout by Heather Westbrook– www.hwdesigns.info

Contents

FOREWORD

I'm sitting in a coffee shop thinking about writing a book. Like all thoughts, the danger is that's all they'll remain— thoughts. We must create head space to allow our thoughts to permeate our minds and draw courage for action and the construction of a new reality. I'm hugely into the concept of "do it now" and have been thinking about writing a book for two years. Time to stop procrastinating and embrace opportunity.

It's just two days into 2014, and many people are making New Year's resolutions. I'm not. I made a commitment to become a better me six years ago and have a personal growth plan in place to guide me. I've set daily, weekly, monthly and yearly goals because the magic happens when you draw a line in the sand and say to yourself, "I'm going to become more."

How do you become more? That can be a loaded question. You start by being intentional about your actions and behaviours, establishing regular disciplines and habits that, practiced over time, will produce a shift in the way you behave and result in a change of action. You continue to monitor and focus on small details with meticulous precision. You protect and nurture your mind, becoming a steward of mental greatness and being fully aware of whom you allow to influence you and speak into your life. You surround yourself with people who are better than you. It has been said, if you're the smartest in your group, you need a bigger group. You raise your standards. You see possibilities in the midst of problems. This is imperative to living a successful life because life throws you curve balls, and you must be mentally healthy and assured. You must find out who you are, and forget about trying to play God.

I have titled this book "Inside Job." This concept was birthed from the profound truth that we're all a result of our thoughts. Everything we are or have started as a thought! God didn't make a car, and he didn't make a table, but he gave us a tree and he put iron in the ground. What are you going to do with the talents God has given you? If we improve our thoughts, we improve our experiences and our life by tapping into new revelations, knowledge and creative genius. How wonderful and exciting!

This book serves as a reminder of how powerful our thoughts can be— we can imagine and create even to the point of starting our own personal revolution and becoming a change agent. Once we understand we can change our thought process, we can change our whole world. This idea exemplifies one of my favourite proverbs, "If you don't change direction, you end up where you are now."

Everyone has a story to tell. I hope mine inspires, encourages, educates and galvanises courage deep in your core. I hope you'll stand up, express yourself and tell your story in turn.

I've just completed my first 5k of the year. I followed this up with a series of leg curls, blanks and dips because I want to lose two inches off my waist, and the only way to do that is to have a plan. The truth is, anything worth achieving will cost you something, and quick wins often are detrimental to our long-term success. When things just fall in your lap, you fail to appreciate them or learn from the process. Our modern, Westernised society is built for instant gratification. Movies on demand, fast food, drive-through coffee shops and the list goes on. Let's face it, there are times when convenience is, well, convenient. But, there's nothing more gratifying than having mud on your face, scraped knees and sweat on your brow because you've spent of your own courage and strength for a cause worth achieving.

So, as I sit here in my local coffee house sipping a white chocolate mocha, the pain I feel in my legs is a welcome one— a result of me pushing myself, aching and sore, but working toward a desired result to benefit my longevity and quality of life. I want to lose these two inches so I can be more active and more prepared for what life throws at me. Too often, we are reactive to this life rather than proactive. We sit back and wait for what life throws at us. You don't have to accept the "inevitable" or take the path society deems "correct." You can create the life you want if you knuckle down, have a plan and execute it. Turn thoughts into actions. Break the trend. Stop the slide. Stop aiming at the target without loosing the arrow. It's time to fire.

Sometimes in life, we pass judgment on those who are successful. We look at their material possessions and become jealous. We want those things. We want other people's fruit but are unprepared for what they went through to receive such luxuries. We don't see what they said, "No" to, what they wrestled with, sacrificed or died for to push through and create a lifestyle of accomplishment.

We're all on a journey to build our castles. The key to getting past the moat and drawbridge is improving the inside of you: Your outlook, attitude and character. Stop comparing yourself to others. Your race isn't against them. Your race is against your potential. To reach your full potential, you need to dedicate every part of your ability to self improvement and surround yourself with positive, high achieving people.

In life, we all have people who are Anchors and Engines. Anchors keep you grounded. They're practical realists. They see the bigger picture and stay emotionally confident. They're dependable and steady. They're meticulous and habitual, and their motto, like the proverbial turtle is, "Slow and steady." Then there are the Engines. They fire you up because they believe they can fly, believe you can fly and awaken your imagination. They know a leopard can change its spots. They have the audacity and the balls to make things happen and encourage you to take action.

We all need a healthy mix of these comrades in our lives. Problems occur when we're top heavy. We have too many Anchors, so we play it safe. We do the "sensible" thing, we embrace routine, we act and behave the "right" way. Similarly, when we have too many Engines, we act before we think, we get burned, we burn out, we think we're Superman, we don't take "No" for an answer, we make more mistakes, we're outrageous and confrontational. It's easy to love Engines more than Anchors. They're charismatic, fun and in constant motion, but as I grow as a man and reflect on my own life I more fully appreciate the Anchors who have slowed me down, taught me to look up and, occasionally, stop to smell the roses.

Like most things in life, the key is balance. I fully agree with motivational speaker Jim Rohn's famous concept that we're the average of the five people with whom we spend most of our time. I take my time and investment in friendships seriously, so I'm forever reviewing and reflecting on my personal associations. It's vital to surround yourself with people better than you. If you're the smartest and most successful in your group, you need a bigger group! It's essential to be acutely aware of whom you allow to speak into your life. Your mind is a powerful muscle. Not only does it need exercising, but it can be affected by our five senses: What you listen to and whom you listen to; What you're watching and whom you're watching; What is touching you and whom you're touching. We need to be great stewards of our minds. Take each thought captive and have such tight security that only after ruthless interrogation do you allow a thought or suggestion to penetrate and either fortify an existing belief or add new wisdom. We allow too many suggestions, temptations and thoughts to penetrate deep within our minds unfiltered. It's not always easy to ruthlessly take every thought captive, but nothing worth doing ever is.

On the other hand, we hear so much in the news about obesity. People, especially children, eating cheap, sugary, fatty foods that cause health problems. It's no secret the body is being fed the wrong thing. However, I'd like to point out another grave concern— mind obesity. Too many people are walking around with fat heads, feeding their minds with poor nutritional content. Your brain is a muscle, and it needs exercising too! As a culture, we allow so much to infiltrate our powerful minds through what we watch on T.V. We watch the news with horror; We read magazines and books riddled with fear, death, adultery and rape. We watch seemingly harmless soaps for fun and yet they're full of the subtle enemies of dishonour, disrespect and sarcasm. Don't get me wrong, I'm all for watching a movie or a show from time to time to help you relax, switch off and do nothing, but make wise choices because your brain deserves for you to be responsible with it. I find it staggering the average person uses only nine percent of their brain. This is at once worrying and exciting. How much potential do you have locked away in there?! We are just one thought away from a cure for cancer. One thought away from a vaccine for AIDS. It's time to protect your mind, and tap into your creative genius.

Ironically, your brain falls into an alpha state when allowed to breathe unfocused. Have you ever wondered why some of your greatest ideas come in the shower or on a walk? We allow our brains to talk to us when we silence the mind chatter, enter into rest and enjoy the moment. Just like when the penny drops, when we are still, we really do tap into our creative genius.

Our world and our lives are so intense, filled with so many responsibilities and demands, that it's really hard to be silent and reflective. With this in mind, I encourage you to find 10 minutes every day to be silent and take stock of your life. Create time in your schedule where you are purposefully silent and quieten the mind chatter. Go for a walk around the block; Go to a quiet room; Or stay in the shower longer to embrace the moment. Protect your mind— give it the space and opportunity to tap into its creative outlets. Make it a habit. You'll thank me for it.

This book isn't just about me encouraging and stimulating you with my own growing pains and revelations. It's also about revealing who I am through my journey. When you understand where someone comes from, you can more clearly understand the thought processes and struggles a person has had to take to get them where they are now. Each of us have our own path, our own allies and foes, tests, obstacles and challenges. We make mistakes, some of which cost us our reputation and integrity. Sometimes, we wind up on the receiving end of other people's choices and mistakes, and it's easy to feel that life has dealt us a rough hand. Some say you have to play the cards you've been dealt, I say, "If you don't like the cards you've been dealt, get a new deck." Stop settling for what others think about you and the way you should live your life! I want to blow the lid off what you are capable of. Don't settle for what others think. For example, why do the "terrible twos" have to be so terrible? In my house, my two-year-old is turning the "terrible twos" into the "terrific twos." Put that in your pipe, and smoke it.

PART 1

#insidejob

Over the past 12 months, I've been using the hashtag #InsideJob on Twitter. As you read this book, I encourage you to take a look at the feed and join the conversation around the topical Tweets. I hope you'll also start using the hashtag to ask questions and build a unique, organic community that leverages the networks in which we all invest and live.

We're all on a journey. If we want to change our lives, our opportunities and the way we live, it all begins on the inside of men and women just like you and me. Long before we become debt free or shed those 20 pounds, we first commit to these thoughts within our minds. We must all become conscious learners and educators if we want to evolve, advance and embrace our full potential.

"Our deepest fear is not that we are inadequate. Our deepest fear is that we are powerful beyond measure. It is our light, not our darkness that most frightens us. We ask ourselves, who am I to be smart, pretty, talented and fabulous? Actually, who are you not to be? You are a child of God. Your playing small doesn't serve the world. There is nothing enlightened about shrinking so other people won't feel insecure around you. We are all meant to shine. We were born to make manifest the glory of God within us. It's not just in some of us; it's in everyone. As we let our own light shine, we unconsciously give others permission to do the same. As we are liberated from our own fear, our presence automatically liberates others."

–Nelson Mandela

Discover

"You don't throw a whole life away just because it's banged up a little." – *from* Seabiscuit

I come from humble beginnings. My parents were working class, and I lived in a place that lacked prestige but embraced a neighbourly community spirit. When you're not surrounded by luxuries, it forces you to fortify and bind together what you do have. Memories of my childhood are sometimes hard to stimulate and, sometimes, difficult and sensitive. I'm thankful that the passage of time and God's grace have lessened the pain I once felt around my broken family. We all have these sorts of battle wounds, some self inflicted and others as the result of others people's actions. I want to be truthful about my past in order to illustrate that you can't experience the joys of life until you're prepared to accept that, at some point, pain and disappointment are part and parcel of it. The problem with pain and disappointment is far too many people stay there— they stay in pain, disappointment and depression. Not me! And not you from now on. Together, we're going to put a line in the sand and make a step toward healing and restoration.

I'm thankful for the battle wounds and struggle because I know the force of our past, when channelled correctly, is our strength and courage in the future. It's no surprise then that studies looking at the life of an entrepreneur consistently find a trigger during childhood that results in a creative, problem solving intuition. I often find when I look beyond the success of a person, they embraced the pain that at one point halted them in their tracks. My childhood was a challenging one. I remember the time my parents decided to divorce. I was 8 at the time, and I was upset, confused and broken. I remember me and my sister comforting each other and discussing what we would do. I faced many challenging days when at times my closest friend seemed to be a pet rabbit even though I had the available support of friends, family and my parents. I felt alone and isolated. While I know now my parents never stopped loving me, and neither of them rejected me or my sister personally, it surely felt like it at the time. I have no pain in my heart anymore,I love them both very much, just a sensitive scar reminding me how brutal this world can be. Today, I can smile and be thankful that I made a choice not to be a victim but to overcome.

I love a good movie that moves people to action. One of my favourites is *Gladiator* and the line, "When death smiles at you, all you can do is smile back." It speaks to me of an opportunity to overcome, to face the stark truth that we live in a brutal world. It may not be physical death we need to overcome, but we need to be mindful of our past hurts holding us prisoner. Life can't be born in areas of death. Smiling upon our struggles shifts our mindset, creates courage and bravery, changes the way we think and the way we perceive our current situation. We must fight for our emotional freedom rather than allowing the past to taint our present and future.

When we experience pain, it feels raw and personal. As an 8-year-old boy, it was hard to process such a traumatic experience and I was filled with sorrow, hopelessness and confusion. But, I'm better for it. I developed character and started to understand my God as a personal father, although I recognize that only in hindsight. I was able to forgive, to move beyond the pain, to have the courage to look up, to make something of life, rather than live as a victim. We can grow beyond disappointment if we can muster the courage to look into our past, look into the pain and be better for it.

You aren't bound by your circumstances, nor do they define you. During a recent talk to a group of business students, I visually illustrated this using a five pound note. First, I lit the corner with a match. Then, I took a pair of scissors and put a little nick in it. Next, I took a black marker and crossed a line through it. Finally, I screwed it up and threw it onto the floor. After each action, I asked the students if the value of the five pound note had changed. They all said, "No." Exactly! People can burn you, they can cut you, they can write you off, they can screw you up and throw you away but, regardless of the circumstances and the things you're put through, your value does not change.

During my childhood, I found comfort and healing in looking out for those who were hurting. I supported a number of charities and raised money for the Hillsborough disaster. It eased my pain when I took my eyes and energy off my own difficulties and looked to contribute in my community. I've heard some say the best cure for pain is hard work. This has certainly been true in my life, but you never face the reality of your difficult situation simply by putting it off or hiding it away. Holding onto pain causes us to hold back in life and stay in our comfort zone. But, we don't grow in our comfort zone— we grow out of it! The enemy of forward momentum is remaining in the comfort zone rather than stepping out of it. All I've achieved has come from entering into new realms of self exploration. Regardless of the outcome, the opportunity to test yourself, harness your skills and sharpen your sword often comes from unfamiliar or uncomfortable situations. Get out of your comfort zone. Discover who you are. Go somewhere you've never been. Explore. Push boundaries. Do something that scares you.

As time went on my heart began to recover, but I did comfort eat as a child and put on lots of weight as a result. My confidence was already low, and I became addicted to chocolate, eating two or three chocolate bars at a time without really remembering. Escapism is what I'd found— a place where I could forget about my pain and bring a quick fix to my broken life. An adult hides behind drink, sex, drugs and other escapism activities, but it's not healthy to stay in the pain! I refuse to stay stuck in pain, brokenness and depression now.

The weight I put on from comfort eating resulted in me being bullied at school. I was called names like "fatty" and really hated school! I had a couple of good quality friends in school who really helped during those difficult times and eased some of the pain I was feeling. I'm sure they don't realise how much their friendship helped me. We often did things together, and that resulted in all of us being called other names. My days and weeks were torturous. It wasn't just verbal bullying I suffered, I was physically bullied too. Remember compasses? They helped you draw an accurate circle and had a sharp end. During class, one lad would throw them into my leg until they stuck out like a dart, causing my leg to bleed. The sad thing was the lad who did this to me was a so called "friend" whom I hung around with after school at times. We need to be mindful of those people in our lives we allow to influence us and with whom we choose to spend our time. Granted I was young, but there's a great lesson here. I spent time with a person who wasn't good for me and clearly didn't care about me. Yet, day after day, I decided to spend time with him. We hear this common theme amongst those who suffer domestic violence. Even though this was negative attention, it was still attention. Being noticed, even for things that hurt me, helped me realise someone could see me after all.

It wasn't until I confronted my enemies that the bullying stopped. I went on a trip with my classmates where we spent the weekend living on a canal barge and learning about the waterways. I bought some souvenirs for my dad and sister. When my bully discovered these, he broke them and threw them onto the ground. This was the trigger that pushed me over the edge— the moment I decided enough is enough. Even though I was timid and lacked confidence, I was furious. I looked my bully right in the eye, walked straight up to him and punched him as hard as I could in the stomach. You might imagine how much emotion and force was in that blow. He fell to the ground and never bullied me again. I'm not condoning fighting, but I would do it all over again— only sooner.

In life we have a choice: Tolerate what people do to us or look them in the eye and say, "Enough is enough." I won't be intimidated by anyone because that's no way to live. Taking action, standing your ground and saying "enough" to the bullies in your life (whether they be other people or your own internal bullies like guilt and shame) are often the only catalysts you need to come into the light and begin the process of positive change. I didn't stay in the victim house. I kicked it down and built my own revolution, and you can too! With a bit of positive internal dialogue, we can turn things on their head and go from being a victim to a victor!

As an aside, I had another turning point on this same school trip when I had a near death experience. Thinking myself clever and invincible, like most 12-year-old boys, and thanks to the recent defeat of my bully, I attempted to jump from the barge onto the dock. But, I slipped right down into the water where I was trapped between the bank and the barge edging ever closer to me. I was at high risk of being crushed to death and caught up in the propellor blades at the rear of the barge. My ancestors were boat builders, and it was almost as though I had a special authority to command the barge to move away from me and not crush me. I remember crying out to Jesus to help me and commanding the barge to move away. Suddenly, it was like the barge was lifted out of the water and abruptly moved in the opposite direction. When I spoke with the captain, he told me canal barges don't naturally move that way, and he believed the controls were taken from him. This was the first time I believed in my heart God had a plan for me. With time, I discovered that more personally than ever before.

Being a teenager is such a wake up call. You go from

having life handed to you on a plate to really having to start taking responsibility for who you are. This is essential to realising life is precious and can be taken away at any moment. It's a significant time for self discovery and also a time when you have multiple choices to make. How are you going to dress? What are you going to study at school? Are you going to pursue a faith or religion? What skill do you want to develop? What do you want to do for work? Do you want to start dating? Do you want to be involved in a sports team?

I often see synergies between sport and business, and both are great passions of mine. It was sport, in my childhood, which had the greatest impact on me emotionally, mentally and physically. I was a football fanatic and spent hours reading football magazines to predict all the scores in the football league. I spent every lunch break playing football with a sandwich or crisps in my hand. I just loved the game, but I never enjoyed playing on the school football team because the majority of the lads were immature and the thought of spending an extra hour or two after school with them seemed like a crazy idea. Instead, I played in the garden with my dad and sister— a much more enjoyable option.

I remember a new P.E. teacher called Mr. Aldridge who had arrived at our school from his birth town of Hull. He was tall and lanky, and his passion and skill was basketball. I had never played the game, but he was encouraging trials and introduced the sport into our P.E. sessions. I enjoyed the frantic pace and team dynamics because I've always enjoyed high tempo sports that require you to think on your feet and aim at an obvious goal. On this occasion, the goal was in the shape of a basketball hoop. I started attending every Friday. Gradually, I started to improve. I was committed and becoming a reasonable player. Mr. Aldridge gave me my chance when, for the first time in a long time, he put his faith in me and made me captain!

That was a big deal to me, actually writing this fills my eyes with tears, because I needed a break. Anyone who knows me knows, if you back me, I will come through and deliver. This was the break I needed.

I love the turnaround events that manifest themselves in your life. I was willing to try something new. I was willing to commit and enjoy a new experience. I was willing to be habitual and attend training week in and week out. My teacher spotted a leader, and I spotted an opportunity that ultimately resulted in the first building block of restoring my confidence. Goodness this makes me want to punch the air. We all have those moments of sheer delight— like when a swimmer touches the wall to clinch a gold medal. This was such a poignant opportunity to celebrate a long-awaited victory. Making me captain was a privilege and one I accepted with great enthusiasm and honour. I ended my school year as the top point guard scorer in our school district, but it also resulted in me dropping those extra pounds. For the first time in my life, I could see my toes! I had confidence. I felt good. I looked good, and the girls came a knocking! Oh, those glorious days of unending possibilities.

Although I was exceptional on the court, I was always in the academic shadow of my exceptional sister at school. Through no fault of her own, Jenny was smart and, as such, well respected by both teachers and classmates. It wasn't fun being compared to my more intellectual sister. I remember a few parent evenings when teachers used to say to our dad, "I wish Mark was more like his sister." I was learning to accept these words as fuel for the fire, to prove people wrong and create my own story and purpose. This coincided with my near death experience and steered me to surrender my life to Jesus, allowing him to heal my heart, comfort me and give me a new identity. I saw an immediate lift in the way I thought and acted, which was further highlighted on the night where your parents go and speak with your teachers about your progress and attention in the various classes you study at school. When my teacher sat down with my dad he said, "Your son is like a different man. He's focused, confident, hard working, and his attitude is exemplary." That felt pretty good and, while I would love to take credit, it was actually a tag team effort for allowing God into my life.

Sport, alongside my faith, enabled me to start tapping into my own innate strengths of leadership, courage and purpose. Things were starting to look up. Through those painful early years, my roots had started to take shape and form. I often found situations in my life where I was able to encourage someone else who was going through a relationship difficulty, a family break up or struggling with a bully. I've always tried to look out for the underdog and champion them, encourage them and surround them with hope and possibility. School was brutal for me, but I'm better for it. Coming from a broken family was heart breaking, but it served me well. It's not your circumstances that define you! I believe when you reach those early teen years you come to a T junction in your life. Your body starts to change, you become more aware, you're finding a little independence, life's becoming more serious, responsibilities and choices are being presented in front of you. It can be both scary and daunting. Likewise, it can be extremely exciting and liberating to start creating the life you want. Over a period of 24 months, I was presented with my first job, my first girlfriend, who I wanted to hang around with, what I spent my money on, what time I went to bed, what I did with my time. I had a world of choices and seemed to successfully navigate my way through the early years of teenage life.

Generally, when you're a teenager, you're not naturally money savvy because you don't yet appreciate the value of money. Many of us are reliant and expectant of our parents giving us pocket money just for being cute.

Thankfully, working for my granddad delivering fruit and vegetables to local hospitality venues at the age of 10 gave me a glimpse of exchanging time and skill for money. I'd always been good with money. My first independent job was working at Woolworth's on the entertainment counter where they sold CDs and videos. I was living at home with my dad and sister and started paying a little rent. I was even able to save a decent amount, and the year the Internet launched I purchased my first computer with dial up access! Do you remember the noise for dial up Internet? Like a small rocket launching into space with some serious hiccups from downing a glass of Coke. I had for the first time achieved something from my own labour. I'd worked hard and made a choice to invest the money I'd earned and bought myself a computer. Wow, money really gives you choices and opportunities! It seemed symptomatic of the current season I was in— the ability to make a choice about where to spend my money and with whom I would spend my time.

My first serious girlfriend came at a Christian camp after I'd played a five aside football tournament. I was walking back to the dorms with some other lads when a group of girls following behind us began wolf whistling. I didn't think anything of it and even joked to the other lads it must be their sexy legs, but the whistling continued. Eventually, one of the girls broke away from her friends, tapped me on the shoulder and invited me to dance with her at the disco planned for later in the evening. I accepted her kind invite, playing it very cool. I remember sprucing myself up and thinking what an opportunity. I knew how to get my groove on a la Kevin James doing the Q-tip in his kitchen in the film *Hitch*. I managed to reign it in a bit and it worked, as we went on a fair few dates after that until the stress of a long distance relationship prevailed. Despite that the relationship ended, it was a great experience— a welcome eye (and door) opener for subsequent girlfriends. During each relationship, I learned something more about myself. Looking back, I'm grateful my teenage years began to ground me and form the foundation of the person I am today— a young man with choice and confidence able to take blows and get right back up.

Today, I know the level of your success is determined by how quickly you bounce back from adversity, disappointment, and heartbreak. Whatever happens, dust yourself off, wipe your bloody knees, cry a river but, whatever you do, have the courage to go again. Don't quit! Dig deep! Lift your head! My childhood was often miserable, awkward and disappointing, but my past hasn't defined me. I've learned and treasured the lessons that have rooted and grounded me with more knowledge, strength and courage than if my life had been easier and blessings had been handed to me on a plate. I'm grateful for that.

My story only becomes more exciting, more inspiring and more powerful from here but, before you see the fruit, you have to wrestle with the pain, the struggle, the tensions, the write offs and the comparisons to others. You aren't running a race against the person to your left or your right, you're running the race against yourself! Your race is against you reaching your full capability, fulfilling your potential and discovering your strengths. Quit comparing yourself to others, and embrace your unique and authentic self.

I left school with 9 GCSE grades. These are the entry grades you need to progress onto college or an apprenticeship training program following high school, and mine were bad. But, I knuckled down in my final year to rescue my qualifications from embarrassment. I'd always been the class clown, loving to joke and make people laugh. My laugh is like that of a hyena who has stumbled across a lion kill— distinctive and infectious and cause for subsequent belly laughs from anyone within ear shot. I'd managed to entertain my classmates to the detriment of my grades. But here's the thing, you can do terribly at school and still achieve enormous success in the marketplace. Just look at people like Bill Gates who flunked school and are so successful they're household names. Of course, this is the exception not the rule, but it should encourage you. Just because you don't have the grades or qualifications doesn't mean it's game over for you. Now, I'm not saying don't work hard and study at school because you need to take advantage of every opportunity that comes your way. But, I don't care who writes you off and says you can't achieve something because you don't have the grades. As entrepreneurs, we find a way. If you can't find a job, make one. Entrepreneurs have a sixth sense about finding solutions to problems.

Although I had the opportunity to go to university, I wasn't a fan of school or of the larger education system. I've always learned by doing and by exposing myself to situations that allow me to take instruction and then be left to interpret and express it the way I see fit. Ironically, I've become such a lover of learning through the last eight years that I've read more books than I had in the previous 24 years of my life. I once read a staggering statistic that 80 percent of students who leave college never read another book in their life time. Maybe I should create an audio book of *Inside Job*?! We have to adapt our product and business to make them accessible to all learning groups and styles.

After a few months working for former retail giant Woolworth's, I was offered an opportunity to take on more responsibility and accepted full-time work as head of the entertainment department. This was my first step on the leadership ladder with the opportunity to progress within the management structure, and it seemed like a decent proposition for a 16-year-old young man living at home. I was even able to walk to work, which was great for my health and my wallet since I didn't take the financial hit of petrol and car costs when first starting out. This enabled me to save like a trooper and start paying my own way.

I embarked on a series of retail management NVQs to help assist me and expand my knowledge. National Vocational Qualifications are work-related, competency-based qualifications usually completed in the workplace and designed for you to gain the specific skills and knowledge needed to do the job successfully. Even at a young age, I was starting to realise I needed to up my game and tap into my personal skills and strengths. Woolworth's was a fantastic boot camp for my work experience and exposure to the real world. The store was situated in a not so pleasant area of Coventry, which had its fair share of crime, violence and robbery, and most of my colleagues were twice my age. Have you ever led people who are more than twice your age? It can be a huge challenge. I was throwing myself into the deep end, but I have many fond memories of my time there. This was the first time I understood it's the people who make businesses. Most people quit their jobs because of the people they work for or the people they work with because it really is the people who make the place. If you're not in the right environment surrounded by the right people, you'll feel the need to break out and find your true environment that brings you satisfaction.

Thankfully, the majority of the people I worked with have been incredibly friendly and kind people, and I totally understood the difficulty of a 30- or 40-year-old adult taking instruction from a 16-year-old. Nevertheless, I made decisions, I made mistakes, I had some successes, I achieved, and I failed. But, boy, am I thankful for the exposure to such a work environment. If you work or have ever worked in retail or hospitality, you deserve a round of applause— it's so under appreciated. As a sector, it's underpaid and misunderstood. You learn how to serve people and how to deal with people's egos. Trust me, when they speak to you like crap at the bottom of their shoe, you certainly develop character.

I often look back at the times I was physically threatened or emotionally abused trying to prevent a shop robbery. It was intimidating and sometimes didn't seem worth the hassle. I often tell people to pick their battles wisely, but I'd become very protective of my store and the people in it. It was my first taste of experiencing a community of people where I actually got to know them on a personal level. Over a period of two years, I was able to start conversation after conversation with regular customers whom I knew by name and also knew enough about them to stimulate more meaningful conversations about their work or home life. I really developed my customer service and people skills during this time. We joked and laughed and sometimes there were some sombre moments, but on reflection they were all playing a part and crafting a culture inside me that has shaped many of my views, understandings, experiences and philosophies. If you want to thrive, you need to place yourself in an area where your strengths can be displayed and exercised, where you're welcome to express yourself and where your energy is appreciated by the people and creates a culture of community.

Interestingly, this opportunity was another confidence booster where someone saw the potential for me to lead and manage. After faithfully serving my employer through hard work, reliability and an energy that built a strong and healthy community spirit, I quickly climbed the management ladder becoming store supervisor and then assistant manager. I enjoyed being out of the store when new shops and retail outlets were being built and my skills were used to implement new store openings and refurbishments using best practices I'd tried and tested. Never let anyone look down on you because you're young.

What you lack in experience, you'll compensate for with hard graft and enthusiasm. When you do what you love, the world conspires on your behalf to make it possible. We must all find what we're good at and then do it with passion, focus and enthusiasm. People will notice. We're all being watched, and that can either scare you to death or excite you to the core. I always let it excite me. You have a choice.

Woolworth's was my first taste of the real world, and it was going well. I'm a loyal person and stick it out long after others had abandoned ship and run for cover. Sometimes I don't know when to quit. It's interesting when you have a little conflict between staying loyal and staying committed, being comfortable in a routine and yet have a burning desire to change direction, to leave the shores of safety and familiarity, to see what's around the corner, to expose yourself to the elements, to test yourself, to risk at the opportunity to conquer and experiment. Over the years my loyalty has been strong, but my burning desire to change, choose and experiment and the desire to be curious again has opened some doors— some good and some bad. The difficulty is not in the options but in the choices you make. I often go with my gut when it comes to decision making. Any big decisions I face, I thoughtfully pray through and weigh the options. I often role play, saying "Yes" and "No" to each opportunity helps me discover how I feel and think toward the situation. It's like trying on a couple of shirts. They may both look great, but once you try them on a certain colour may enhance your features or drain the colour out of you. One may be tight or baggy or have short sleeves and the other long. When a decision comes in the form of choices, I consider each option mentally and even say out loud "I am going to be on the radio" or "I am going to be on T.V." taking note of the way each one feels. It really helps bring clarity and understanding to your predicament. It helps me process, and it will help you too.

An opportunity presented itself right out of left field. I wasn't expecting it or planning on it but, in the midst of my work success, I began to fall in love with a girl. Falling in love messes with your head! My problem (and I seemed to make a habit of this) is that I would fall for girls who lived a whole ocean apart from me. Guess I like to do things the hard way. So, I was presented with a choice at only 18 years old— a world of possibilities, a call to find my own path, a curiosity to find my own identity, a desire to discover who I was and what I was about or stay stuck in place. I had no financial responsibilities, so choices weren't so cut throat. I'd been living with my dad and sister. I had a steady job I was progressing in. I walked to work. I had a decent amount of friends. I participated in many hobbies. I had no debt. I had a car that got me from point A to point B. Most teenagers don't experience some of the luxuries I had until much later but, true to form, I've never been happy with the comfortable path.

My childhood taught me, regardless of what comes, I can roll with the punches. I can and will bounce back, reflecting on what's the greatest risk in making a decision. Simple self reflection can often give you the courage to be bold and brave and forge ahead with a positive outcome. There's no greater enemy to your life than indecision— sitting on the fence, letting opportunity after opportunity pass you by. That's why it's vital you know who you are and what your passion is. When an opportunity comes along, it's too late to prepare. You need to be prepared. I was ready to step out and leave these shores of safety. This time around it was in the form of packing my bags and doing something I'd never done before— leave home. I wasn't just leaving home to move a few streets away. I was uprooting and traveling to the United States of America— the land of the free! I was flying out to Michigan to be with my girlfriend. After initially meeting online and meeting in Toronto, we decided to see how the relationship would build and grow when living in much closer proximity. This is really the time in my life when I made the switch between boyhood and manhood.

Imagine

*When you do what you love the world
conspires on your behalf.*

I remember the day I left the shores of the United Kingdom filled with lots of questions and uncertainty. But, love has a way of grabbing you by the boot straps and giving you the boldness and courage to step out. That's why it's so important we fill our lives with the things we love. We don't always know the ending to the story but we can start any story we want— over and over again. I'd never been away from home more than a few days, so this was going to be something new and enthralling yet uncomfortable and uncertain. I knew nobody in Michigan other than my girlfriend. I was 18 years old and packed my bags like I wasn't going to return. Maybe that's why I was interrogated when my plane landed— immigration questioned me as to the purpose of my trip due to my open ticket raising a few questions. I can't say that was the welcoming I was hoping I would receive from a so called ally country. I remember boarding the plane with a lady who had all the similarities of Julia Roberts whom I had met in the airport lounge prior to our flight. It was quite the upturn compared to the timid and shy character I'd embraced during my childhood and teenage years. With new vigour and swagger, I'd become more confident during my time working in a customer facing environment. We had a natural rapport and it felt pretty good being 18 and this lady having 10 years on me! If this was anything like my foray into the United States, it was going to be a pleasant one. Even now, on reflection, I have a big grin on my face.

Incredibly, the older woman had just left her partner of 10 years. He had all the wealth in the world, and she had everything a woman could dream of— the kind of lifestyle most would snap your hand off for. She shared how she'd become a house wife with a husband who was a very successful businessman with high expectations and old fashioned views of the world. He wanted her to cook him meals and iron his shirts while he stopped her from going out and prevented her from getting a job and expressing herself. This is as clear a case as any that money doesn't buy happiness, and a controlling man only ends up alone. If love isn't motivating you and driving you and those around you, it doesn't matter what substitute is placed In front of you because it doesn't have the stamina to go the distance. As human beings, we all look for genuine love in the people we care about. If the relationship becomes predictable, we owe it to ourselves to mix it up and resuscitate it.

How fortuitous that she was ending a relationship, and I was embarking on one. We were coming from different stages of life yet relating on a common level. Whatever life holds for us, we must take control. Sometimes that comes in the form of surrendering. It doesn't seem to make sense, but sometimes we have to give up things for new seeds to be planted and encourage new growth and opportunities. I can't keep up with all the times I had to give something up before something new came my way. Remember, good can sometimes be the enemy to great. When making decisions like that, you have to keep your brain active and your eyes wide open. Over the course of the seven hour flight, we engaged in chit chat and some deep conversations about purpose before she asked to see my passport to compare the differences to her American one. To both of our amazement, we had the same birthdate— October 16th!

The flight was a pleasant one, and we made good time with a tail wind right behind us pushing us on. I was both excited and apprehensive at the prospect of seeing my girlfriend and starting a new chapter in my life. I'd given up my position at Woolworth's to make this step. I'm very much an all or nothing guy, and I tend to fly by the seat of my pants and step out before thinking. With age and wisdom, I've certainly become more calculated with my decision making; However, I still enjoy the buzz and adrenaline of taking a risk knowing my God is bigger than any mistake I may make.

When I finally proceeded through customs, I was greeted not just by my girlfriend but a whole bunch of her friends too. I'd spent months apart from my love and was looking forward to that moment of passion, but I had to wait and my reaction to that fact was mixed. Despite the wait, I actually met the most incredible, inspirational and passionate man whom I call my best friend even to this day there in that airport lobby— Mr. Joel Rodriguez. There are not many men in my life I would stand up, salute and applaud for all the countless times they've told me what I need to hear rather than what I wanted to hear. We all need people like that in our lives. If you don't have anyone like that, you need to make finding one a priority. Sure, it's painful at times (especially when you need to be offended to wake up and smell the roses). Joel has had my back and my trust since the first moment I met him. I had just endured a seven hour flight, had been bombarded with questions from U.S. Immigration and just wanted some food and my bed. I had four suitcases in tow, and Joel greeted me and instantly took my bags. We'd never before met though he had heard about me; Nevertheless, he honoured me and served me in a way that to this day sticks out in my mind. We all have special memories that seem just like yesterday— you can remember the time and the place, colours and sounds— well this snap shot in my life was one of those for me. Honouring people has the power to uplift others and results in lifelong friendships.

One of the things I love about America is its people. Americans get a rough press from certain parts of the United Kingdom— labelled as arrogant, obnoxious know-it-alls. I have to refute this on the grounds of my experience with the wonderful people who live in the United States. Of course, like any country, there are the fair share of idiots and buffoons, but I love the culture of young men and women who address their elder as sir in a sincere and honouring way. Being called sir as an 18-year-old young man was unfamiliar. But, rather than feeling awkward and embarrassed, I felt empowered and uplifted. It resulted in me reciprocating with positivity and honour. I became quicker to listen and slower to speak. I started observing and was caught up in a wind of gratitude and respect for my fellow human. America and its people had an instant impact on me.

It was extremely beneficial for me to be introduced to another culture. Only six months prior, I'd experienced Brazil— from celebrating a carnival atmosphere in a major metropolitan area, to witnessing extreme poverty in very deprived areas. I helped open an orphanage, which was very sobering. These two different experiences and cultures were shaping me, teaching me to take my eyes off what I don't have and focus on what I do. I quickly realised if I was going to be rich, I was going to be rich in character and in the relationships I held dear. The most valuable assets in our lives and businesses are our people. It's all about relationships. Invest in people and your bottom line will increase.

My U.S. girlfriend was part of a youth group and the leaders of the group kindly opened up their basement to me. It had only recently been refurbished, and I had my own bathroom, shower and living quarters. They didn't charge me rent, which I offset by helping with various chores like cutting their large yard and, occasionally, babysitting their son. Seemed like a fair deal to me. Far from the pomp and bravado of a people who are called arrogant and obnoxious, they'd opened their home, made me a guest and gave me all the privileges of a family member.

I was enjoying spending time with my girlfriend and began to build a rapport with Joel. I'd always been fortunate to have a guy in my life that I had shared lots of time and thoughts with, and I was grateful for the opportunity to strengthen my bond with Joel and get to understand more about his thoughts and way of thinking. We could talk about anything without judgment.

I've already shared how in life and particularly in my first 18 years, I experienced "suddenly" moments. Not always positive, not always negative, but altering my course of direction. The reason I'd given up the comforts of living with my dad and sister and my reasonably well paid job is because I believed the grass could be greener on the other side— that I needed to explore the love I had for a woman and to see if this was a woman I would spend the rest of my life with.

Within a week of me being there, we decided it wasn't working. I remember on that Tuesday morning being down in the basement all by myself, rocking in a rocking chair, balling my eyes out. My heart hurt. It was a strange experience because, while I was most definitely upset and disappointed, I also felt a release inside myself. It made me lift my head and believe the purpose of my trip to the United States wasn't about love but about self discovery. Who was I? What was I about? What was my purpose and my identity? This sent me into a tail spin for some weeks, fully out of my comfort zone, not knowing anyone well after being in the country for only a week. I was staying with people I didn't really know. I wasn't working. I felt isolated and vulnerable, I could have got a flight home, chickened out, went back to my comfort zone, but I didn't. I waited, I worked through it, and I embraced the pain and the confusion.

After a few days my heart was still raw, but I'm not one for moping and feeling sorry for myself and the days started to have purpose. Luckily for me, Joel was in between jobs, which enabled us to spend more and more time nurturing and building our friendship in a relaxed environment. My days started to consist of a number of house chores in the morning, followed by cutting a number of gardens for neighbouring houses, corresponding with family and friends over email and fixing myself some lunch. The afternoons were incredible, I was kindly loaned a car, and I went to the beach every day! For the whole duration of my stay in the United States, I played volleyball with a group of Albanians and Mexicans and finally got some colour on my white English skin (I'm not one of these people who allow the weather to determine if I'm going to enjoy my day, but sunshine really does give you a lift and a buzz). I played volleyball between 1-4pm before meeting with Joel or other friends with whom I was establishing a connection.

I wasn't a hermit, but those experiences and difficulties were a great training ground for my adult communication. I know what it's like to hurt and the temptation to wallow in self pity. With this in mind, it empowered me to reach out to others. I know what it's like to feel isolated and cut off, but now I'm extremely confident and can connect with most people. I'm enjoyable to be around (if I do say so myself), and being around people energises me and gives me a sense of purpose.

When I reflect on my relationship with my now ex-girlfriend, I still have huge fondness and gratitude. While the relationship ended and, at times, looked bleak and not always positive, I'm so thankful for what I learned about myself. I know at times she provoked me with her friendly and flirtatious nature around other boys, but I took the bait because I was battling jealously and insecurity issues. When my parents divorced, I feared being rejected and cut off. While I can now acknowledge the divorce wasn't a slur on me or my sister, it felt that way at the time, and this was just what I needed to finally break free. Unless you can cut yourself in half, you can only physically be in one place at a time and children are caught in the middle. So when my parents split, we had a choice to make— remain a victim of divorce or use it for our own advantage and self discovery. I was afraid of my girlfriend leaving, rejecting or hurting me. I knew in my head that I needed to trust and hold her with an open hand rather than one that controls and manipulates. I tried my best but, at times, I failed miserably. I was so scared of losing her that, in the end, I did. I don't believe jealousy was the main reason we split, as it was a reluctantly agreeable decision, but I am thankful for the role she played in my life. It enabled me to deal with some deep heart issues, find some healing and perspective and grow bigger than my problems.

Sometimes you win and sometimes you learn. In this case, like so many cases in life, if you have the character to reflect, regardless of pain or failures, you can always find something to learn from and change your view, your understanding of who you are and what's important to you. Reflection is the biggest tool to personal growth I have found. I reflect on each meeting, every task and relationship. We all need to be so careful whom we allow to speak into our lives and with whom we associate ourselves.

In the end, I'm proud I stuck it out in the United States. I didn't take the easy route out but stayed with it and the U.S. did become the land of the free. I became liberated. The man in me was born, and the boy was put to sleep. It's incredible when certain events change the fortunes and directions of your life. This was certainly one of them, and one that would stand me in good stead for years to come, reminding me life had become a world of endless opportunity and exploration.

Men were born to be adventurous and explore. Adam, who was placed in the garden of Eden, tended and explored his land. He tested boundaries and became curious until curiosity got the better of him. In many cases, you hear quotes like, "Curiosity killed the cat." While curiosity can get you in trouble, I think our lives are too predictable. We like routine and religion and comfort, but it comes at a cost of never exploring or experimenting and never exposing yourself! I want to wage war on routine in my life. I want to see what's around the corner. I want to keep exploring and pushing and challenging the status quo. I may get burned and make mistakes, but you can't really live and embrace this life if you're not willing to look beyond yourself and understand the power of your mind.

After a three-month season of self discovery, pain and confusion, my life started to settle and opportunities started to present themselves. As my friendship with Joel grew, we became infectious and contagious with our larger-than-life spirit and, together, soon befriended many people. We spent countless hours in and around the mall, where Joel (who was half Mexican and half American) often cheekily asked for the minority discount. This was something only he would have the nerve to ask but, in most cases, he was granted a discount. On some occasions, I'd also receive a discount for my cute English accent. Talk about using what God has given you. I'm sure I wouldn't have that kind of favour now in such an economic climate but, on reflection, those moments made me chuckle and remind me that if you don't ask, you don't get. Yet, we rarely have the nerve or audacity. I like when people are audacious and ballsy. When you are, incredible and surprising things can happen. But, a word of caution, be careful what you wish for because you may well get it.

After a few months apart from my ex, my heart was beginning to recover. On the odd occasions I would see her at the group meeting in the basement where I was living, the pain wasn't as intense. The relationship had helped me to discover who I was, and some of who I was wasn't nice. It was controlling, insecure and jealous. I made a conscious decision to move on— to be thankful for the pain. Some will never know the pain of a break up or a failed relationship. I'm grateful I gave of myself truly and honestly and, by doing so, felt the pain and disappointment of separation. It's inevitable in life. Suck it up, and then spit it out. Even today, I never view my failed relationship as a failure. I learned so much, I experienced so much and I was better for it.

One day while I was at the mall with Joel, I caught the eye of a young lady who was working in one of the outlet stores. Aware of my current situation, the soreness of my heart, the mix of emotions and self discovery, I was readily mindful of not wanting to conjure up romantic feelings. I was acutely aware of the stereotypical rebound approach in relationships, and I respected my own heart as much as anyone else's not to be overly moved by my initial response to catching this lady's eye. I guess knowing I was allowing myself to be open to such a reaction was a sign my heart was healing, and I was free to once again be brave to expose my heart to the highs and lows of acceptance and rejection. In all honesty, I'm unsure if I confided in Joel in this moment of exhilaration and excitement. I remember exchanging a "Hello" and "How are you?" with this new young lady. We exchanged smiles and both went about our day. It was like coming up for air. During these few months, I had been holding my breath, and this little reprieve was good for my soul.

Subsequently, and through a number of intriguing events, friends of friends, parties and gatherings, I met this new girl again at a Hawaiian themed party. I was donning a grass skirt and a wreath of flowers around my neck. I would like to think it was my legs being exposed that made an impression on her but, in all honesty, the impression I made was actually a negative one. She had shared that when she eventually retired (she was in her 20s at the time) she would reside in New Mexico. Since I was quite spiritual at the time, I replied, "Does God want you to retire there." She was suitably offended, seeing it as a knock on her dream. That was never my intention. While we're talking about intentions, I've come to know and battle with the consequences of having good intentions yet still causing pain and difficulty and challenges in my life. It's important to have good intentions, but that alone is not enough and can still cause conflict and pain. I had offended her, but I was unaware. Sometimes people have to be offended in order for their heart and attention to be arrested. It wasn't the approach I was looking for, and I wouldn't suggest you go and offend the one you're pursuing. But, if you do, don't be overly concerned. It certainly got under her skin and made her ponder and chew on the fact I'd thrown in God's direction for her life.

One of the keys to my own success as a young man was the ability to be persistent. If I really wanted something I went hard after it. To this day, when I hear "no," my mind interprets a "yes for later." I think the more failure and disappointment you've had, the more hardy and tough you become. You can more easily shrug off set backs. When you have a clear understanding of who you are and truly like yourself but others don't take to you, you see it as their loss rather than yours. I've always believed if someone doesn't like you or want to spend time with you, you're better off without them. It's a wonderful place to be— to know who you are and be comfortable in your own skin is where life really begins. When you persist and live a life of consistency, people begin to understand who you are and what you're about. When others know what you do and understand the way you think, opportunities materialise. People want to know your secrets and find out your story.

I was up this morning at 3:30am to partake in a live radio

broadcast in California, which was being aired live at 8pm PST— the equivalent of 4am for me. There was a young lady of 23 who phoned in and professed her desire and plan to be an entrepreneur. But, she didn't have the people around her to encourage and guide her. In fact, they were doing just the opposite, pulling her down and being dismissive of her ideas. I listened and encouraged her to find new associates who would encourage her, challenge and stretch her so she could be all she wanted to be. It's so important we surround ourselves with people who are positive and create an environment that helps us grow, be inspired and have the courage to tap into our own creative genius. These people help us take it from thought to reality. On reflection, I've had a decent friendship base for some time— often with people five or more years older than I am. Over time, my associations have greatly altered, and I am finally settled on whom I share my time with. I mention this because who you allow to speak into your life affects the way you think and, subsequently, your behaviour.

When I had offended this new girl, it wasn't my intention. Typically, I may have felt misunderstood and almost rejected from her response, so it was of great encouragement that I didn't react with insecurity on this occasion. Instead, I held my nerve and let the occasion pass by. My intention was a good one even if the execution was off. It didn't stop me reaching out to her and, eventually, we met night after night down by the Blue Water Bridge in Michigan that connects the United States to Canada and all its various borders. It was refreshing to speak with a woman about the cares of my world— those things that bothered me, but which I was afraid or ashamed to share or reveal to someone else. She was a great listener. We spent hours, often into the small wee hours of the night, talking. I found it strange and liberating we were connecting and it wasn't based on a romantic state. We genuinely bonded as friends and confidants in each other's lives.

Every time I'd built a relationship with a girl previously, it was instant romance and the normal rush of hormones, but this relationship was built differently. This one was built on friendship, honesty and trust rather than attraction, chemistry and lust. After numerous visits back and forth across the ocean for both of us, we married on May 24, 2003 in Croswell, Michigan.

Looking over this significant event in my life and the countless highs and lows of my story so far, it occurs to me that it really helps if you love roller coasters because they're full of twists and turns and unexpected loops and dark places that cause you to experience the emotions of both terror and extreme excitement. That's exactly the outlook you need in this life. Sometimes you win, and sometimes you learn. Regardless of what you go through, always ask the question, "What did I learn from this?"

Ironically, I'm not a fan of going upside down, so I refrain from roller coasters. I like some order. I like to keep my eye on the horizon; However, mentally, I'm a fan of the roller coaster. It's vital you're aware that both facets of life will come at you and people who are not prepared tend to get stuck in a situation or circumstance for which they're not prepared. That's why it's key to develop your attitude and character. I see a person's real character often on a sports field because it brings out the fight and the passion in you. I've seen the quietest and most assured characters come to life in the heat of battle. When intense pressure comes into your life, how do you respond? Are you calm and calculated, or are you rash and easily provoked? Whether you have a little or a lot, whether you succeed or fail, keep your feet on the ground and don't allow the emotional highs or lows to knock you off course. Stay steady. Of course, celebrate your successes and mourn your losses, but move on. Don't live on yesterday's crumbs when you can have today's loaf. Don't let anything knock you off course. Take regular readings, create and protect time to think and invest in you. There's so much noise and distraction out there in this world, you must stay centered and focused on your mission statement, understanding your key reason for being on Earth. Once you've found that, then it's about building a structure and support network that nourishes your brain, your relationships and attitudes.

I had my new wife as my sounding board. She was always the one who listened, encouraged and kept me centered. Who do you have in your life that can bring those qualities to you? If you don't have someone like that, go be that someone to someone else and you'll find everyone wants to be your friend!

When I arrived back home in the UK, I knew I had become a man. I had made decisions and choices, and I'd allowed myself to dream and act on those dreams. In Proverbs, there is a verse that reads, "Do first things first. Do your outdoor work and then build your home." I'm not sure I have a full grasp on exactly what that means; However, I knew before I built anything of worth and sustainability, the foundations had to be right. I needed to get myself straight before I could even think about establishing my own home and family. I have always wanted to be a leader. My ah ha realisation was that the first step to leadership is leading yourself. In many cases, leading you is harder than leading anyone else.

I arrived back home with a small debt, but my dad kindly let me move back home, and I picked up a job the day after my arrival at a new local Italian restaurant. I always knew I was good with people. My background working in retail gave me enormous confidence, and the lure of tips was a massive one. I had around £1,000 worth of debt from my stay in the United States, and I was determined to eradicate it. When the restaurant called to let me know I had been successful in the interview process, the manager told me my jovial personality stood out against my khaki pants. They were hiring people of character, and they certainly got one with me.

I told my dad the news, and he was rightfully pleased. But, he didn't think the role suited me and that I wouldn't stay at it more than a couple of weeks! Talk about a boost to my confidence dad haha! Typically, that could have played on my mind and messed with my head. I'd always looked up to my dad to inspire and encourage me and, to be fair, he often did just that. Unlike previous responses to a lack of confidence coming from others close to me, I was able to roll it off and prove my father wrong. I know, for my father, it was more a question of the job not suiting me, rather than my capabilities. Regardless, I rather like being the under dog. I love when people write me off, say "No" or doubt my ability to a task or situation. I have a great ability to "make fuel for the fire"— to take what someone says toward me in a negative way and turn it on its head to launch me forward. Incredibly within the first three weeks of me working at that restaurant, I paid off that thousand pound worth of debt and bought a new car.

The restaurant was roughly three miles from my home, and I walked there and back after each shift, which was great for my waistline and my mind. But, goodness, after being on my feet all evening and following that up with a three mile walk, it was gruelling and challenging. It resulted in late nights. After a few months, I was accustomed to my new way of life. Going to bed at 2-3am and waking at around 10am suited me. With my wife living in The States and being five hours behind, I often called her after my shift to catch up.

When my dad returned from his holiday with his new wife, he saw the new car, and said, " I take it you're still at the restaurant and doing well." He was surprised and liked being proved wrong. I told him I'd paid my debt and had some rent money for him. It's so important in life, if you want to get ahead, to over deliver. Go beyond what people expect, add personal touches, create some shock and awe moments and prove people wrong— not for their benefit but yours.

After a few months, I'd established a credible reputation as a waiter, but the pinnacle arrived when guests started to ask the door host to seat them in my section. This goes back to my previous point of over delivering and being personable. If you own a business, it's key to be authentic and create a culture that is sincere and empowering.

Being a server in the restaurant industry is one of the most demanding but eye opening jobs in which you can work. You're delivering a service. At times, people treat you with little respect, acting demanding and assuming. People tend to speak down to you, but showering someone in kindness is the quickest way to defuse and challenge an individual to take note of how they address and speak to you. I had reasonable success with this approach. Some guests would soften and, quite frankly, some were shocked. I always liked to give my guests enjoyable and memorable service.

Within the industry of hospitality and other similar sectors, it is paramount you create positive memories and create a theatre experience. Long gone are the days when people just throw some food into their mouth. They want something extraordinary, and I liked to think outside the box to create these moments. I would often observe fellow colleagues wait on their tables and ask myself what I could do better. It became a lot of fun. Attention to detail is key. The ability to read body language, being sensitive to the person or people meeting together. Are they in a hurry? Do they want peace and quiet? While the hospitality industry can be unforgiving, the processes and struggles, demands and obnoxious people you come across, it is the battle ground to help you deepen your understanding of customer service and how you can build a business on details by simply being more attentive and authentic than those around you.

I worked faithfully as a waiter at the Italian restaurant for 12 months before stepping back onto the management ladder. I didn't make this step because I wanted a more influential role. I made this step because I wanted a mortgage and, regardless of my 12-month history of tips, I was unable to convince a mortgage lender of my regular income. So, I decided to make the step and take a guaranteed salary. Current statistics reveal the average age in the UK to get on the mortgage ladder is the mid 30s. I was grateful and thrilled to make that step when I turned 23.

Over a period of five years, I'd taken on further management roles at various companies, building my experience, challenging my management and leadership skills with some failings and some successes. I worked for branded and unbranded hospitality companies. Some stretched me and some frustrated me. I'm thankful for each place I've worked because each helped shape me and reminded me of the kind of person I want to be (and the kind of person I don't want to be). We all have a past. We can't go backward and alter any of it. For some it's pleasant and for others it's painful. Regardless, you can put a flag in the ground right now, and I shall do the same. Yesterday finished last night. It's time to take your past and let it launch you into your future. I had to take a series of steps to start creating and stirring up opportunities in my life that were in line with my passions and strengths. The more true and dear you hold yourself to your own abilities, the more attractive you become to those around you— especially the market place.

We all have trigger moments in our lives, and I remember mine very clearly. I was working at a historic attraction in the UK looking after a series of restaurants and food outlets. I was making progress in my career and project managing a number of key initiatives. I felt stimulated as opportunities to show off my skills were becoming a regular occurrence. Half the battle is giving someone a chance to grow and seize an opportunity. Some people just need some encouragement and an avenue to express themselves. If you can create opportunities for your team, I guarantee morale (and productivity) will greatly improve. Start showing some faith in those with whom you work. Create a stage and watch them perform!

I'd always desired to have my own business. My late grandfather Bertrum Ernest Sephton was a serial entrepreneur. We lost him when I was only 18, but I'm sure I would have greatly benefited from his wisdom, failings and successes as a businessman. The one thing I know is that he had a great reputation. Your reputation is the greatest and most valued commodity you have as a business owner. Lose that, and what do you really have left?!

People have varying opinions on whether entrepreneurs are born or made. I'm happy to let that one ride, but I do often hear of the entrepreneurial spirit being passed on. If that is true, in my family, it seems to have leaped right over my dad's head— or maybe he's just a late bloomer. I've also come across a common theme when speaking to countless entrepreneurs about their history and childhood— many of them can recall a traumatic and difficult time during their younger years. Due to this, they recall turning to problem solving and risk taking. Maybe when you face so many problems as a child, you either decide to let them bury you or you become a specialist at problem solving. A big part of being an entrepreneur is finding problems and offering solutions. Maybe that's why crisis seems always to be in an entrepreneur's timeline. While acknowledging the deep desire to create and build something, finances were an issue for me. I never had much debt, but I'd never really kicked on beyond having enough money to live within my needs. I had some savings but certainly not enough to invest and give up a well paid full time job. I remember one night, after a particularly long day, I turned on the television and came across a woman called Dani Johnson. Dani was different, and her message was infectious and powerful. It was almost like Dani was jumping out of the T.V. screen and speaking right into my heart.

Dani was talking about marketplace ministry, finding what you love and bringing it to the marketplace. It was clear Dani was a visionary and blazed her own trail. I was captivated and hung on her every word, as I began to feel empowered and inspired. I knew Dani was based over in The States, but I had never seen or heard of her before. To my utter shock and excitement, she announced she was coming to London for the first time later in the year. It's funny, in life we often think, "I can't afford that," but the only words going through my head were, "I can't afford not to go." As soon as tickets went on sale, I booked my seat and invested most of my savings on this two-day event. I believed Dani had the blue print to unlock the missing piece of the jigsaw puzzle for me to take my desire and create my own business that I'd previously not had the knowledge or tools to make a reality.

During one-to-one sessions with one of my senior managers at work, he often asked how I was and showed an interest in me as a person. He was a good boss, and we can all learn a lesson here. Many of us are surrounded by managers, but we're not always surrounded by leaders. Managers are operational. They manage a process, procedure documents and uphold operational standards. They ensure you're paid and have the equipment to do your job effectively. Leaders, on the other hand, develop people. They focus on improving your skills and attitude. They nurture and create an environment for you to establish yourself in your industry. All good companies need a mixture of the two.

Most companies I've worked for are packed full of good managers. Audits look good, standards look good, businesses are profitable, but they have no soul because they have no leaders who care about their team and cultivate a culture of honour and belief that fosters a space for people to thrive. Thankfully, on this occasion, my boss was both a manager and a leader. While he wobbled at times between the two, his act of kindness has stuck with me through the years. I doubt very much I will ever forget this kind gesture.

A strength of mine is that when someone does me right, I never forget how they made me feel. One of the aspirations I have in my life is to liberate and provide opportunities for people to make something of themselves. When someone has put their faith in me, championed me or blessed me, I don't forget. I want my life to be one of generosity, purpose and influence.

During that one-to-one meeting, I shared with my boss how this weekend I was heading to London for an event where I was going to develop myself. Being the sort of man he was, he was intrigued and encouraging. He asked me if I had sorted accommodations. I told him I had but had to put it on my credit card since I had spent my savings on the event itself. He looked at me and said, "I will personally cover the cost of your hotel room for the two nights you spend in London." Wow! For me, that was a big deal and a kind gesture. It was an acknowledgement of support and gratitude. I've never wanted to be a passenger in this life; I've wanted to drive. Far too many people in our society are back seat passengers in their own life and don't realise they can jump in the front seat and take control of the wheel to change course. This kind gesture was a huge financial and morale boosting act of kindness, and I headed to London with more excitement than a kid on Christmas Eve.

I travelled down to London the night before because I didn't want to rush. I wanted to give myself (and my mind) the best opportunity to take in the information, be focused and ready for what Dani was going to share. I rose early the next morning (around 4:30am) and went down to the lobby to queue for entrance into the large conference hall. Since seating was on a first come first served basis, it was to my delight when I discovered I was the first in line. I knew the value of sitting on the first three rows because I'd read you take more in if you sit on the first three rows. You feel more engaged and part of the atmosphere and environment. You feel more connected to the speaker and are able to better gauge communication and eye contact. I knew if I was investing my money and time, I wanted to get as much value as possible out of it. Whether it's true or not, I've never retained such focus and excitement as I did during this conference. It's important to have expectations because your brain remains active and your eyes open to possibilities. You're ready to learn and seek out new revelations as your mind becomes pliable and soaks up key information and knowledge like a sponge.

Dani covered a lot of ground that day. There were so many nuggets, ideas, tips and inspirational materials. I could write a whole book on my experiences just on that day in London. Dani shared two key, yet simple, messages that launched me into action and onto a journey of personal development and discovery. These two effective adjustments in my mind and thoughts helped trigger new behaviours and created situations where I started to take control of my destiny.

The first point Dani shared was if you increase your skill and abilities in the marketplace, you will increase your value. If you increase your value, you will demand a higher fee for your services and skills. Very simple, yet profound. For the first time in my life I knew if I wanted more, I needed to become more. Wow! Exciting!

The second point came as a result of a five minute Q&A session. Another perk of being on the front row is that I had the ability to grab Dani's attention by being in her line of vision. I shot my hand up instantly, and Dani acknowledged me and asked for my question. I proceeded, "I believe, Dani, that one day I shall have my own business. I believe it's God's desire for me. I don't have a great deal of money to invest, what should I do?" Dani went on to explain that less than 1 percent of people in the UK were millionaires. Of that 1 percent, 98 percent of the millionaires made their money based on land and finance. Dani shared that if I did have money to invest, it would be wise to invest in these two areas. She continued and shared the second place you can invest is in stocks, but with stocks you can win and lose. In summary, I know you don't have the funds to invest in either of these, so you only have one place you can invest in. Dani paused and drew my anticipation. The only place you can invest is yourself. Incredible, yet so simple.

Even now, I want to punch the air in celebration of these words, as it was these very words joined with my improving skill and ability that has resulted in a personal development journey over the past seven years! Incredibly, this journey will never end. When you stop learning, you stop growing. These words challenged and liberated me, Dani focused me on playing to my strengths and exploring my passions, improving and investing in those areas that would give me fulfilment and new opportunities. I started to believe in myself and the ability to change the direction of my life— no longer hidden in the shadows and average, not trying to please everyone, not being labelled or stereotyped, but liberated to be me, unique and authentic, creating a life I love by being engaged with myself and fully aware of my capabilities.

When I was heading home on the train, I felt excited and invigorated. I picked up Dani's book *First Step to Success* out of my bag and started to read each page with great focus. Incredibly and sadly, I'd only ever read one book from front to back before this moment, but I knew if I wanted my life and opportunities to be different, I needed to introduce some positive habits into my life. One of them was going to be reading. Have you ever read or heard something you felt was just eloquently written for you?! Well, that's what happened. Dani was sharing her story and, through storytelling, engaging my heart and emotions and encouraging me to take action in my life.

In the book are a series of principles and strategies that have shown proven results in the marketplace. Since I was still employed but in the midst of carrying a huge desire to create my own business, I knew I had further lessons to learn before branching out on my own. I've always embraced a very teachable spirit and this has enabled me to harness every morsel of wisdom and knowledge in each situation. Over subsequent weeks and months, I searched my heart and carried out various personality exercises to help focus on my key strengths and those places in my heart that gave me enormous satisfaction.

People development and building a community that can dream and act on its dreams was very much at the forefront of my passions and desire. Over the years, I'd developed a huge love for people. I love encouraging people and strengthening them in their pursuit of happiness and life fulfilment. I love to champion and encourage and even, at times, challenge them to think bigger, act smarter and take some risks. Life can be as dull or as enthralling as you like it. When you allow your mind and thoughts to have a voice and create a platform to think and reflect, you feel liberated and fired up. I knew, at this point, I needed to invest on improving my natural skills and desires and enrolled in a series of Open University courses to fan the flame and increase my level of understanding and curiosity. Personal mentoring and life coaching were very much a part of those skills I developed. I worked with a number of mentors and coaches who all brought their own ideas, mindsets and philosophies. My dad used to say, "Eat the meat, and spit out the bones." Regardless of who you are working with or the environment you are in, there will be some that's good (the meat) and some that's bad (the bones that look to choke and impede your breathing). If you don't like what you hear, then spit it out. It's your prerogative.

I began to invest in myself. I was reading and listening to inspirational and educational material. As Zig Ziglar said, "I travel in my automobile university vehicle." I started to fill my mind with good wholesome content. I started disassociating myself with those who were not good for me to be around and made new associations with people who took action, dreamed big and were successful in multiple areas of their life. I was aware that if you get rid of the garbage, the rats would go too. My mind was too fragile, too powerful and too intricate for me to not take better care of it. Being mindful of what I looked at and whom I listened to, whom I allowed to speak into my life was (and still is) of great importance to me. There are so many voices and opinions, so many paths and ideas, but you have to be a good steward of your own mind. If your head is a mess, it's a clear sign you have not been stewarding your mind and making wise decisions that fundamentally impact on the the way you think, act and behave.

I knew the importance of with whom I associated myself.

I started doing some research on local, successful entrepreneurs and found out where they spent their time and chilled out. I found a nucleus of them went to a local spa and gym, so guess what? I went ahead and subscribed to a gym membership. Often, conversations start in the hot tub, and I started to get to know these super successful men and women in a more personal way. I totally agree sales is like farming rather than hunting. When you feel hunted by a sales person, you run away and hide because you can smell their BS a mile off. But, when you genuinely engage with your client and seek ways to serve them, invest in them and take the time to find what makes them tick, you develop trust.

I don't get to know someone because I want something. I get to know them in the hopes that I may learn something and, in turn, give them something to unlock their roadblock or creativity. I like to get inside people's heads so they can consider a different way of thinking and operating. I never engage in business talk with anyone to start with. It always begins with trust through casual conversations with meaning and purpose. It's really important to make yourself intriguing. Don't give all your secrets away. People like to look, but don't play all your cards because curiosity is still the number one component of successful marketing. Encourage all new connections to see you for who you are.

At first, I held back. Since I was holding back, these successful men and women started to ask questions about my life. What my dreams were? What I was currently working on? I began to share my desire for business. That I was investing in me. Incredibly, over a four-month period, I had a little mastermind group in that hot tub of super successful business people who were more than willing to encourage, advise and instruct me. I respected them greatly and, while I didn't agree with some of the ethical ways in which their businesses were built or how results were obtained, I loved their wisdom and knowledge. That's the way to do business. Get to know people. Be intriguing. You might be surprised how quickly people will start asking questions and will want to help you because you didn't ask for it. Super successful people are wary because all people want is to take, take, take. I've had the privilege to get to know some very influential people in particular in the sporting industry because I looked at the ways I could serve them, not what I could get from them. Who can you serve and be a friend to? Whom do you admire and value? Great, now go and serve them!

Creating an environment and staying in the wind of those who are influential is a great place to be, but it starts with servanthood. Eventually, you will notice they actually enjoy your company and pick up a thing or two from you too. To be a person of influence, you must not seek fame but, instead, seek to be of service. I am extremely grateful for my experiences as a waiter. It taught me the act of service, attention to detail, creating memories and positive experiences. It wasn't all rosy. As I've said previously, some people talk down to you but you serve them anyway. In the end, it says more about you and your character than it does about the customer.

I've heard people say they don't do sales or are no good at sales. Truth is, we are all selling who we are or something we do. Have you ever had a job interview and got the job? Then, you sold yourself. Ever had a boyfriend or a girlfriend? You sold who you are. It doesn't have to be the stereotypical sales role to be sales. We live in a society where we are all being watched— where we all want to be liked and accepted. Don't you care about how you come across? I do. That's why I listen to people and, regardless of the outcome of a conversation, I take time to reflect and ask myself what I've learned. Whether it's my 4-year-old son or Richard Branson, I have the mindset I can learn and serve to achieve something amazing— trust.

During my months at the spa, my opportunities and mindset began to grow. I'd taken the words of Dani Johnson to heart. It was vital to invest in myself and increase my skill because increasing my skill makes me more valuable in the marketplace. When your value starts to go up, your influence follows right behind. I was hanging out with people who were better than me. They'd journeyed beyond my footprints. I stopped meeting with people who were not good for me, my mind or my desires. I decided I have no time for dream stealers or for those who suppress my thoughts and feelings due to their own insecurity and laziness.

I began reading books! Who would have thought that? I didn't like reading at all. I started studying. I invested in a mentor. I went to personal development seminars and workshops. If you want to grow, you have to be intentional. Occasionally, we grow out of an accident that makes us evaluate our priorities and make subtle (or sometimes radical) choices to make life more meaningful. Thankfully, these accidents don't happen too often. Why not take control of your life and have a personal growth plan? I have a budget I put aside to develop me— books, audio, magazines, qualifications, mentoring, seminars and conferences. Feeding my mind, helping it flex and grow, to feed a continual habit that opens the windows and doors of opportunity before me.

I was amazed when I started to apply the principles of Dani's book to my life and current job that I began to create and seize opportunities. My line managers noticed a shift in my mindset and behaviour, Within two months of reading her book and applying the knowledge to my life and mind, I had clinched a promotion and increased my salary. One of the shifts I made was that my boss was no longer my Earthly employer or my line manager, my boss was my God. With that in mind, I began to work unto him. If my manager never saw the good I did during a project or difficult situation, I was confident my God did. I stopped seeking the approval of man and started to work solely unto Him with incredible results. Regardless of whether you believe in God or not, making the shift to have a level of excellence regardless of someone noticing or not enables you to ride the highs and the lows and keeps you stable with your feet planted firmly on the ground.

Often, when we go through seasons of change, we develop and evolve. It wasn't long before I needed a change of scenery and a new challenge within my career. This move coincided with my Open University courses and, in the same month, I switched employers and launched my business part time. It is very common to set up a business part time as you begin to transition yourself away from employment into self employment and then entrepreneurship. It reduces the risk and allows you to build the foundations with financial pressures reduced.

I am not advising everyone take this route. I've come to see the value and power of deadlines and pressure when you have no choice but to make your business work, rather than staying in the comfort zone and assurance of a full-time salary while you embark on your own part-time enterprise. I really want this book to empower you, so you are able to make your own choices and play to your strengths. You'll know which one feels right for you. You just need the courage to step out and do it.

Over a period of of six to 12 months, the transition was starting to take place. I had a few clients I started to coach and mentor and was thrilled to be doing something I loved and getting paid for it. I also plugged myself into a network marketing business to create multiple streams of residual income. We should all have at least three streams of income that are not based solely on our time and current action— that's the beauty of network marketing. You can do some work from months or years ago, and the payments roll in month after month. Like an echo of your previous hard work and graft, it supports you in the leaner months. Find a business where you believe in its product or service.

When it comes to juggling a full-time job and part-time enterprise, there comes a tipping point. Something has to give. A risk has to be taken. Nothing is certain in this world but death and taxes. If you truly want to put a dent in the world, you have to embrace the uncertainty, and with that comes great excitement and trepidation. People owe it to themselves to express who they are. What better way than creating a revolution of themselves through their own business. I finally made this step. I branched out, and I served notice on my current employer. I had done my ground work: Business plan was in order, accounts were set up, budget was tight, I knew my break even point, I applied for grants and sourced funding from local business hubs to assist me financially in those early months. I continually worked on me, that's where the magic is and the chapters to follow will bring you the value of my own thoughts and philosophies, offering you strategies that can stimulate you to think again, dream again, act again and achieve again.

Achieve

Being excellent today allows freedom tomorrow.

PART II

CHAPTER 1

Entrepreneurship

The ability to take a thought and put it into action.

I recently opened up a discussion during one of my radio show broadcasts on whether entrepreneurs were born or made. This question stimulated a lot of opinion and healthy debate. Some people were insistent entrepreneurs are born and others were certain entrepreneurs were made. In the end, there seemed to be a good case for both. After the discussion had concluded, I went to the cinema to relax and unwind. About half way through the movie, which was unrelated to the subject of entrepreneurs, my mind began to focus on how a caterpillar is born and then transforms into a butterfly. This process could easily be applied to the earlier debate of how entrepreneurs come into being. For me, my paternal grandparents were entrepreneurial. My parents, on the other hand, have always been employed by a company and haven't had the desire to create a service or product in the spirit of entrepreneurship.

Research has shown that many entrepreneurs had problematic childhoods. From the previous chapter, Imagine, you can see that this certainly is true in my case. Combined with my entrepreneurial family history, there seems to be at least anecdotal evidence that I was born with the entrepreneur seed and certain situations in my life made that seed sprout. My experiences in child and young adulthood taught me to fend for myself, grow up early, become self sufficient and look at ways to solve problems by facing them head on.

Remember my bully? I drew the line. Now, I seek others whom I can shield and stand up for.

I'm convinced some people carry the entrepreneurial DNA but die without ever expressing it. Maybe we all carry this DNA but, until we're stimulated by a situation that presents an opportunity for that chrysalis to be formed, we stay conformed to our environment. Stuck or, simply, unaware of the limitless opportunities. In that way, it makes perfect sense that the entrepreneurial spirit may also be cultural. Take, for instance, the United States. Its citizens often are very receptive to opportunity (especially those in the creation business) because the U.S. culture was built to encourage and provoke the entrepreneurial lifestyle. It is then no surprise that lots of creative ideas and startups come from countries like the United States and others with similar cultural values.

In the end, the answer to whether entrepreneurs are born or made isn't a pivotal one. If entrepreneurs are born and that DNA is already inside you, then you better grow up fast and nurture your personal development. If, on the other hand, entrepreneurs are made, then you best begin exposing yourself to an environment that stimulates you, makes you strong, creates opportunities to problem solve and expresses your creative mind. We must all do what we can to allow our creative abilities to express themselves before we reach an age and time where we cannot fulfill all that is within us. Answering these questions will help guide you to finding the environment which makes you come alive and gives the greatest chance for your entrepreneurial spirit to be born. The chapters ahead are a call to action to discover a different mindset and cultivate a culture of empowerment to birth within you your amazing authentic self.

The upcoming chapters teach you and encourage you to listen to your heart and thoughts, to reflect and take notice of what your mind is saying and step into environments that nurture and strengthen your drive and skill.

CHAPTER 2

Personal Revolution

Be you. Everyone else is taken.

We each have a unique gift and purpose to bring our own personal revolution to the world. We are not bound like a tree that can go only as far as its roots will reach. We have a world of opportunity to express, conjure and create incredible ideas and game changing products and services. We were built by a Creator and within each of our creations, in turn, is the very essence and heart of the one who formed us into being. If you've ever made anything, you'll know what it feels like to have expressed yourself— your thoughts, emotions, concepts, beliefs and philosophies. Our products and services are often a reflection of who we are and the journey we've been on because we were created by design— not default.

No two people are the same. We all have our own distinct fingerprints. We're unique, which is why the motto "Be you. Everyone else is taken!" is so liberating and true. The desires that lay deep within you— those dreams, hopes and aspirations— are in there for a purpose. They aren't there by mistake but were placed within you as a representation of the Creator who formed you. You were designed to create something— not just consume someone else's creative idea. When we create, we discover ourselves and come alive.

Take note of those things you desire to experience and express— the desire to open an orphanage, chair a football club, write a book, perform on stage, be a millionaire, be an Olympic gold medallist. None of these are by accident or by coincidence. They're there for you to discover, explore and move toward your deepest adventurous desire. An eagle was designed to soar above the clouds, not to be on the ground strutting like a chicken. Its very desire to fly is based on how it was designed. As a human being, we're designed to achieve incredible things. It's the pursuit of your desire that will get you there. Those thoughts you have about doing something and being something incredible are within your DNA. You were designed to succeed, to accomplish, to fly. You were not designed to be a chicken eating seed and winding up on a Sunday afternoon dinner plate. You were called and created by a unique design to take hold of your future and craft a life that embodies your design and is fuelled by your desire.

Challenge to Action

- Be courageous in the face of mistakes. What mis-takes have you made that you need to look at in the eye and evaluate?

- Face your fears. What areas of your life are para-lysing you to make decisions?

- Start small. Start by making small decisions like what you should have for dinner. When you make decisions (even small ones) you're building a habit of empowerment.

- Set boundaries. When we have all the time in the world we procrastinate. Get in the habit of holding yourself accountable by setting deadlines.

- Just do it. Each morning, I say the words "Just do it" 50 times. When an opportunity arises (maybe running in the snow), you'll find your body running before your mind can talk you out of it because your brain is programmed with "Just do it."

- Find a mentor or success buddy. Sometimes, we need to consider the opinion of others and we all need accountability. Seeking council is wise, but never override your gut if you feel you should go in a different direction.

In order to bring a clear distinction of who you are, one of the exercises I do with entrepreneurs is a personal branding exercise similar to mind mapping. Asking simple questions and paying attention to the answers forms a beautiful mosaic of words and descriptions that embody your true character— the things you love, the words and situations that resonate with your spirit and soul. It doesn't just strengthen who you are and what excites you, but it gives you a fantastic tool (and sometimes provides much needed revelations) when deciding what opportunities you accept into your life. Using a personal branding exercise as a framework to better decision making focuses on energy rather than time spent.

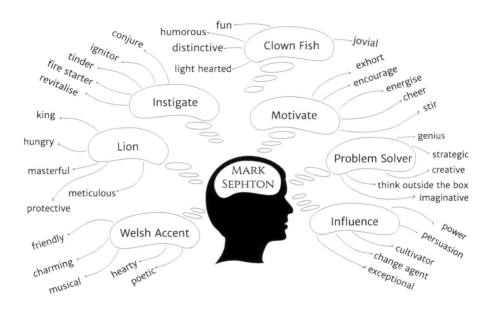

CHAPTER 3

Bread for Your Head

*Far too many people are back seat
drivers in their own lives.*

Ours is a world of endless opportunity, and that's exciting. No one of us has to be a passenger, distant and purely reactive to what life throws at us. Let's turn that on its head: What can we throw at life to ignite a flame of passion and excitement that liberates not only you but those around you? It's a great question. Far too many people are back seat drivers in their own lives. I encourage you to undo that belt buckle right now and jump into the front seat in the car of your life. Put new coordinates into your mental GPS system and start to become proactive.

Most of the opportunities life holds for you already exist in thought form within yourself. They may be laying dormant deep within your soul because your personal history, pain and disappointment has kept them hidden, but when we stifle and hibernate our deepest dreams and desires, do we really live? Life can be bitter sweet. I'm not suggesting life will always be easy, but I want you to be prepared for what comes at you out of those doors of uncertainty. I want you to be ready, with your brain engaged and eyes open, if something hits you in the face. I want you to be fully conscious to make mistakes and choices and decisions fully aware without the temptation to hide behind excuses. To do this, your senses must be clear and your decision-making well thought out. This is why I don't drink. By all means have a nice glass of red wine or a cold beer to celebrate and reward yourself for a week well done, but be mindful that whatever we consume in excess will change and alter our decision making.

CHAPTER 4

Focus

Life is a marathon not a sprint.

I am sat in my local coffee shop watching the people pass by. I love people watching. It fascinates me to watch people's behaviours and expressions in response to things they see, who they are with and how they communicate with others. This particular coffee shop is located in back of a local retailer, and I've counted numerous people who have come into the store just to get to the coffee shop. So many of them initially intent on that perfect cup of coffee are easily sidetracked and distracted by that cute little dress or pair of shoes. That's why businesses pair up. That's why retailers have coffee shops at the back of the store. They know if someone comes for coffee, they may well end up spending some time on retail therapy.

Sometimes, in life, we need distractions to consider opportunities that come from left field, but in a world full of distractions, sometimes when you set out for a cup of coffee, that's all you should return with. Be aware of what you want because indecision is your enemy. You need to empower yourself to make the right choices to showcase your passion and skill. Rather than being reactive and impulsive, be calculated, purposeful and intentional. The next time you have five minutes, I challenge you to spend it people watching. It will help you and your business and may even put a smile on your face.

Challenge to Action

- Find opportunities where you can function individually to bring the meticulous focus you have to the fore and reap the benefits with minimal accountability.

- Create time to write down your desires, and reflect on them often to feel more in control of your life.

- When you establish goals, ensure you include timelines and boundaries. They'll give you clear proof of the progress you're making.

- Allow yourself permission to turn down opportunities not aligned to your key skill set, passions and personal mission statement. This will help protect your efforts toward the most essential priorities and keep you on point.

CHAPTER 5

Sleep, R&R and Timeouts

Breaks lead to breakthroughs.

Entrepreneurs at startup businesses are working longer hours than ever before. They rise early and work late into the night. It consumes their minds and drains their energy. One might argue that a business is like a baby— needing round-the-clock care and investment. This is true to a degree. You have to work at it, and it needs your attention and investment. But, there is danger in pushing too hard and becoming tired. Tiredness and sleep deprivation result in poor decision making. There are some recent examples of this that perfectly illustrate the cost of poor decision making caused by lack of sleep. In fact, the latest BP oil spill was the result of key personnel not having enough sleep and operating with detrimentally impacted decision making. Sometimes, even decisions we make with the best of intentions can wind up being a degree or two off the mark, and the results can be catastrophic.

I work with a variety of entrepreneurs with varying backgrounds, skills and businesses. Something many of them have in common is they're all going 110 miles per hour. They rarely come up for air, slow down or take regular pit stops. Even Formula One has pit stops to refuel and check the safety and performance levels of the vehicle. These pit stops ensure a driver finishes the race and increase the chances of victory. Sometimes, these pit stops are completed in under one minute, but the best ones are usually preplanned. Just like a race car, people need pit stops because scheduling breaks is essential to staying at your peak potential. Occasionally, emergencies and unforeseen pit stops are required— the tyre has blown, there are problems with steering, an oil leak has sprung. These things require immediate attention. You can't ignore problems. If you do, they only have the potential to increase exponentially and result in further complications.

Entrepreneurs often do not carve out regular breaks or take time to reflect, unwind and enjoy the fruits of their labour due to their busy schedules. They feel guilty for taking time out or believe the competition will overtake them. I'm not advocating blown deadlines but, as we discussed earlier, your competition isn't against other people but against your own ability and potential. You will not only protect but absolutely increase the reputation of your brand by coming from a place of rest, recovery and focus and by taking care of your sleeping behaviours and patterns.

Olympians spend countless hours training and exposing themselves to various gruelling conditions to strengthen their mind as much as increase their strength, power and speed. They often rise very early in the morning, they are habitual and regimented, and they start with the end in mind. They are meticulous in creating everyday habits to keep them centered. But, they also take extended periods of time to rest, recover and replenish the liquids lost through sustained periods of hard work and exertion. They know the power of rest. They work with tenacity and drive because they are fully aware it requires recovery to reach the pinnacle of athletic ability.

One of the reasons startups fail is the inability to pace themselves. To work with tenacity on the back of a regular rest or pit stop is paramount to the survival of your startup. You need to allow your mind and body to rest and sleep. Often when we take time out, we tap into our creative genius and have some of the best revelations. Protecting your energy by letting off the gas and reducing your speed is the way to get ahead. Just as a Formula One motor car would be ruined and unable to function to its full potential racing around with a flat tyre, people can't function when they're sleep deprived. This is what many people are doing because they feel that if they're moving, they're getting ahead. That's a business myth that needs to be busted immediately, as it's seriously impeding and destroying lives and businesses. Here on in, schedule time to rest, switch off and refuel. Sometimes the way to get ahead is to slow down, take stock and consider your position and current performance.

I've just come back from a week-long break in the Nottinghamshire town of Bleasby and Horspool. Before the year begins anew, it's paramount you schedule time in your calendar throughout the year to have some downtime: Take a vacation or just stop and assess your life and current endeavours. I never feel guilty about taking a break; However, I do rue the momentum that's lost in the downtime. I understand why so many plough through. If you're an entrepreneur, you most likely love what you do, so it often doesn't feel like work. Unless you actually schedule time out, you will fill every hour which God sends your way, right? I must confess, I love what I do and fill my professional life very full. But on reflection, 80 percent of my current endeavours play to my strengths and harness my passions, while the other 20 percent does not. I'm negotiating to rid myself of those duties that no longer stimulate my passions or give me an opportunity to flex my skills. Breaks and downtime are the perfect time to think on such things.

When it comes to taking a break, you have to think longterm. On my recent break, I walked a bunch, I had more time to read and relax and just switch off. My biggest challenge was quieting my inner voice and the noise of social media (in particular Twitter where I speak with hundreds of people each day). I was able to swim, have a lie in, spend time with my family and children. Being a city man, it was refreshing to breathe in the country air and I used that enthusiasm to go for a run past rolling farms with cows, sheep and pigs. It was the first day of spring and everything seemed new and green.

There was a slight wind, the sun was shining on my face, and I felt invigorated and free. Vacation time is good for the soul. It's like sleep, some need more than others, but it is essential to properly function, to keep you healthy and create stamina so you can function throughout the year.

Life is a marathon not a sprint. It's no good being the richest person in the graveyard. We can't just simply work, work, work— even if it is enjoyable and profitable. You have to be responsible to your own mental health and the mental health of those who rely on you like your spouse, children and employees.

As an aside, I was hugely impressed by Bleasby and Horspool. The hospitality and sense of community was refreshing. I can only applaud the nature of their warm invite and ability to be communal and personable. If we want to make a difference in other people's lives and in our businesses, we must embrace the acts of servanthood and community. We must build a platform that embodies the fullness of what a community is— support and a common purpose that pulls together in one direction to protect, guide, aid and bring nourishment through relationships, resources and networks. If we want to leave a long-lasting legacy and make a genuine impression on those we interact with, we have to shift focus off of ourselves and onto those around us. When you look out for others and share your wealth, people will turn around and share their wealth with you.

It's time we changed the culture of our society and economy by embracing the spirit of community within our homes, our businesses, our cities and inside ourselves. We don't need anymore outward experiences. We need experiences that impact our insides, touch us with honour, and make us feel like we're something special, appreciated and valued. Stir up a spirit of community. Build a network and culture that really looks at supporting, uplifting and blessing those around you. I would never have experienced this if I hadn't taken a break to slow down. When you do good it will come back to you pressed down, shaken together and running over. I am grateful for my pit stop, but it's time to fire up the engines and go full throttle again. That's what a break is for— to get you ready to kick on again. We don't function well on empty fumes, and we harm our reputation when we push ourselves beyond what is healthy and simply sputter along to the finish line.

CHAPTER 6

Positive Habits

Make the mental shift from problems, obstacles and excuses to solutions, thanks and gratitude.

In life, we all need to introduce positive habits to continually draw out the best of us. They keep us focused, help us aim higher and stay intentional to our personal development. For example, I've always struggled to be patient. I want everything yesterday but, as I have grown and matured, I've started to become more rounded and relaxed and realised not everything would have been beneficial if I'd achieved it straight away. Instant gratification wouldn't have helped me value the process or experience a sense of accomplishment when I overcame adversity and dug deep to resolve myself to achieve something of importance. My strongest traits are manifested in persistency and an unstoppable mindset, but patience is a minefield I still battle regularly. Generally, I do and then think, but this has shifted as I've become more wise- though I still like to get things done, test myself and challenge my current levels of skill and understanding.

One habit I introduced a few years ago was the daily habit of gratitude. Each night before I go to sleep, I reach into my bag, pull out my red gratitude book and write a minimum of three things I've appreciated about my day— perhaps a compliment or achievement. Some are more personal and others more generic. When you live in England, and it's a sunny day, that's something to be grateful for! The amazing gift of gratitude is that it shifts your mind from what you don't have onto what you do. When you focus on what you do have, you create an abundance mentality. Having a sense of abundance enables you to share of your wealth in a way that liberates others and causes your mind to come alive to the world of possibilities around you.

Far too many people don't take measures to stimulate a gratitude mindset. The incredible action of gratitude welcomes more excitement and reward into your life. I've found the more grateful I am for my life, for the provisions

God has given me, for the people who have invested in me, the more positive stories and actions I witness. It's a cycle of positivity. Each Sunday I review my week. I look at my wins and losses, as well as those areas that need my attention and those golden moments where I think, "'Wow!" I need to add that into my life or business. This is when I consider my gratitude moments. On a weekly basis, I average 24 gratitudes. When it comes to reviewing my year on December 31, I'm blown away by the gratitude and abundance in my life. When you see that in black and white, it makes you sit up, straighten your shoulders and take a deep breath. My year was a fabulous one!

On reflection of my weekly gratitudes, my most successful weeks in terms of performance were created when I generated the most gratitude. Of course, more success results in more appreciation, but the more you are grateful and thankful, the more people want to give to you because they know you will appreciate it. We all know when you give something to someone who does not see the value in your kindness you become discouraged. The awesome thing in life is you're not responsible for their actions— you're only responsible for yours. If you haven't already, go out right now and buy a notebook where you can reflect, review and focus on the positives of each day— even when your day seems like it's been a miserable one.

Everyone has bad days. I vividly remember a day last year that was a real stinker. I was scheduled to take my sister-in-law to the airport so she could catch her flight back to Pennsylvania in the United States. I'd noticed a small bulge in one of my tyres. Since I was travelling a couple of hours on the motorway, I wanted to have the tyre replaced. I took my car to a local garage but was unable to find the wheel nut to remove the alloys from my car. The only way they could be removed was to physically break them off. I declined hoping to find the wheel nut.

The whole process resulted in my sister-in-law missing her flight and having to take a coach to Heathrow. Once she was on her way, I took my car back to the garage.

The point is, I thought a routine change of tyre was straight forward. Most garages have a due diligence policy where they check the full condition of a car before starting any work. Once my car was elevated into the air during this process, it was clear I needed two tyres and not just the one. Tyres are not cheap, especially around Christmas time, but that wasn't the end of the story. I also needed an oil change, and I had a fog light out too. When it comes to your car, you have to make sure it's safe and roadworthy (remember the Formula One pitstops?). I sanctioned the repairs and, £250 later, my car was back on the road. I'd spent five hours waiting for the work to be done and, by the time I arrived home, it was 3pm. It sure did feel like a waste of my time and money, and sitting down that night to write my gratitudes was more challenging than normal. But, in retrospect, I had so much to be grateful for. My health. That a day like today won't be like tomorrow. That I was able to get my car to a garage rather than have it break down on the way to the airport. When you look at it that way, it's easy to see that it's time to shift from problems, obstacles and excuses to solutions, thanks and gratitude.

Try working with the following list to begin your gratitude journal:

GRATITUDE

Three incredible people in my life are:
  1.

  2.

  3.

Three awesome things about my home and where I live are:

1.

2.

3.

Three incredible things about where I work and what I do for a living are:

1.

2.

3.

Three great gifts of unique talent and skill I have been given are:

1.

2.

3.

Three fantastic gifts of knowledge and experience I have developed are:

1.

2.

3.

Three ways I have experienced blessings in my life are:

1.

2.

3.

CHAPTER 7

Love Mondays

When opportunity knocks, it's too late to prepare.

It's Monday, which means most people are fed up, tired or misfiring. Monday is viewed as the enemy to many— the day that breaks up a nice relaxing weekend, socialising and drinking wine. It's judged like an unwelcome guest or a late night knock on the door. I understand that Monday feeling when you're in a job you don't enjoy and the alarm clock goes off and you have to bribe yourself to get out of bed and face a job you dislike with people who make it difficult. We can all play that game, focusing on the problems rather than the opportunities (see the chapter on Gratitude). There's certainly nothing worse than feeling like you're living a lie and deciding how a day will go before it's even begun. But, you're undermining your opportunities and productivity by writing off Mondays!

I love Mondays! Honestly, I believe whole-heartedly that the success of your Monday helps determine the success of the rest of your week. I love Mondays because it's a chance to reset yourself, recalibrate and set yourself up for success. I rarely schedule any meetings on Mondays unless I believe it's essential to my future success. Instead, Mondays are dubbed "Mark Day." It's a chance for me to be quiet, focused and reflective. I read and educate and stretch my mind. I review my goals and set strategies to maximise forthcoming responsibilities and meetings. I fuel the fire of passion within me. I create headroom to be able to listen and allow my mind to express itself. Mondays are great for journaling too. I ask God to guide me, to give me wisdom and strength. Look at Mondays as your secret weapon to get ahead and stay ahead of those who simply allow Mondays to happen to them.

This habit has been crucial to maintaining my own efficient energy levels and ensuring I'm on the right track and continually heading in the right direction. The danger with not checking in, constantly reflecting and reviewing your internal compass is you can very quickly find yourself miles off course. You may even have spent days, weeks or months believing you're heading in the right direction but failed to look up, evaluate your surroundings and discover you're quite off track. This is why I'm standing up for Mondays! In fact, mine are often so productive, I look forward to them.

I was speaking to a gentleman on LinkedIn recently and we were discussing Mondays. As a result of this conversation, he decided to introduce some positive experiences to his office staff each Monday. What do you know, this new habit left his team energised and motivated for the coming week! He even decided to pay his colleagues on Mondays. That is genius! If you don't have the opportunity to carve out a whole Monday just for you or change around whole office structures, that's okay. You can still reflect on the myriad little things you can do to reintroduce focus and buzz back into your Mondays. Remember, it's essential to the success and momentum of your week. Be strategic with your Monday experiment. Change your personal culture and allow Mondays to kick start your week rather than short circuit your looming responsibilities.

With that in mind, success often comes when you look at how everyone else is following a trend and then create your own revolution and go your own way. Following the crowd often results in ordinary and encourages predictable results. Blazing your own trail welcomes in the extraordinary. It's certainly not for the fainthearted. There is associated risk and you could fail big but, as an entrepreneur, it's worth the risk.

Ask any passionate surfer, and they'll tell you that some of the waves they catch are breathtaking and awe-inspiring but totally frightening. If you don't catch the wave just right, it can bury you. It's certainly a safer option to just hug your surfboard on the seashore, but that ensures you won't get the big payoff. The alternative is to grab your board, wait for your opportunity and turn the risk into a massive momentum–busting revolution of opportunity.

Reflect on your current habits and attitudes. Do you play it safe or do you risk leaving the safety and comfort of the seashore? Do you dare to venture out? The key is patient expectation. You don't want to take a risk without wisdom to back it up, so you need to be prepared. When opportunity knocks it's already too late to prepare. So, get yourself together, have your eyes wide open and your brain engaged. When your big wave of opportunity arrives, you can seize the day. A big wave may come on a Monday, are you ready for it?

Mondays really are "Mark days" in my life. It's an opportunity for me to feed my mind, giving bread for my head and ensuring my week comes from a place of strength, clarity and high energy. Below is my Monday ritual. It's really about setting the right foundation to give your week the greatest chance of success. We can only invest in people and endeavours from a place of rest and vision.

My Monday Ritual

- Journal and pray about my coming week
- Reflect on the week just gone (meetings, new contacts, business relationships, etc.)
- Review my gratitude journal and the goals I've achieved
- Read something inspiring for 20 minutes
- Schedule my week around my passions and energy
- Listen to an educational podcast for 30 minutes
- Check Flipboard for industry news
- Write for 30 minutes about a thought or idea I have

CHAPTER 8

Value

*Small victories today will change
the course of tomorrow.*

I've always said anything worth achieving is going to cost you something. Where is the value of something just falling into your lap? How will you achieve or discover anything? Of course, we all dream about things dropping from the sky, including success, but this is just a fantasy. Some of my greatest memories of achievement have come through long nights, failings and struggles. I'm always encouraged when some things in life are harder to cultivate and engineer. Sometimes, it's better not to force things to happen and allow things to happen organically instead. A stimulating environment and personal culture create opportunities and give us a greater chance of progression and success.

Coupled with my daily gratitudes, I constantly look for new ways to introduce positive habits to increase my productivity and make a shift in my mental GPS. These often manifest themselves through a physical change. For example, I look for triggers that can launch a small new habit to improve my performance. Every time I go to the bathroom at home I get down and do 10 press ups. Have a look at your life and make note of the things you do on a regular basis. While brushing your teeth you could squat or think words of affirmation over your life. When you're in the car, you could listen to something educational or inspirational. When you put your socks on, you could thank God for what he has done in your life. Use daily tasks and chores to create a trigger to a small new habit and, over time, these habits will become second nature and result in an upturn of success and health in every area of your life.

Create these habits to leverage your success. Slow and steady always wins the race. Sometimes we can talk ourselves out of making improvements in our life because the desired result seems like an unattainable mountain. It seems unrealistic and requires more fight than the energy we have to muster. Break it down. Keeping it measurable is the key to the compound effect and eventual success. If you want to tone up, doing 10 press ups every time you go the the bathroom will get you to that goal over time. Don't be discouraged by the size of the end result. Rome wasn't built in a day. It was built brick by brick, moment by moment.

I have a five- and ten-year plan and always start with the end in mind. Of course, the danger in this is when you're constantly looking at the horizon you can neglect the opportunities right in front of you. I'm a big believer in being present and working within the here and now. In addition to my long-term plans, I also schedule 10 daily goals to keep me focused and intentional for the day ahead because once today is done we can't get it back. Small victories today will change the course of our tomorrow. Work diligently with what you have in your hand. The nuggets I share throughout this book are tried and tested by many entrepreneurs who explored or implemented the thoughts, attitudes and reflections that will give you the biggest opportunity to tap into your fullest potential, unlock new heights and attract greater opportunities.

Value is the importance, worth, or usefulness of something. It takes time to stimulate value. To live a life deserving of importance and worth takes consistency. It is a continual journey of improvement and discovery. If we want to become people of value, we must offer more than that which is expected. This comes from us raising the bar on our own standards and abilities to execute at the highest level.

How to increase your value

- Over deliver
- Become an expert
- Take on increased responsibility
- Build impactful relationships

CHAPTER 9

Balance

When we try to burn the candle at both ends,
we're destined for trouble.

Over the past few weeks, I've been experiencing trouble with my physical balance. It coincided with the aforementioned break to Nottinghamshire where I spent time swimming and generally spending excess time in hot tubs. If you've ever had a problem with your balance, which is the result of a problem with your inner ear, you'll know how distracting it can be. It can even keep you from performing every day tasks like driving and walking. The feeling of being at sea leaves you both nauseated and disoriented. Who would have imagined crystals in your ear could become misaligned and cause such an upset to your basic functions?

Often in life, we can be out of balance. We often think of work-life balance getting out of whack and causing issues to your health and relationships. Illustrating this point through a physical manifestation helps flag up the need to ensure we strive for balance in our life to avoid instability. When we lose our sense of purpose, we become top heavy. When we try to burn the candle at both ends, we are destined for trouble. We must give equal measure to the eight key fundamentals which make up our basic DNA:

1. **Relationships**
2. **Family**
3. **Lifestyle**
4. **Mindset**
5. **Business**
6. **Financial**
7. **Spiritual**
8. **Physical**

Each area needs to be balanced, and each area needs investment. When you stop investing in yourself, you stop advancing and succeeding. Our lives need both order and purpose. Success has a full component of those key fundamentals. Success is about being at peace with yourself, knowing how and whom to invest in, there is no point being the richest person in the graveyard. Nobody on their death bed will look back and wish they had spent an extra hour in the office. They will wish they had developed key relationships. The seriousness of finding a balance to fuel your desires means sustaining and appeasing those around us whom we love and who appreciate the time we invest in them.

Before the recent issues with my physical balance, I had taken it for granted. Now, I'm doing all I can to restore it to its normal state. I wasn't trying to disrupt my balance. I was swimming, relaxing and enjoying myself. Sometimes, our balance is affected by seemingly innocent decisions, yet our life's balance is off kilter, and we find ourselves investing in the wrong areas of our lives. Having the wisdom to know where to invest, spend time and even reduce time we spend on an activity, relationship or business venture is an important skill to maintain balance in our lives. We must discover our purpose and vision and work to eliminate from our lives anything that negatively affects our internal compass. When you regularly take time out, be still, evaluate and reflect, you'll more easily be able to assess your balance and determine your equilibrium.

I've learned about a procedure called the Epley manoeuvre, which is basically lying on a bed that tilts you a little upside down where your head is moved gently to encourage crystals to re-align themselves. It's certainly something I am going to give a go. In life, sometimes our world must be turned upside down for us to regain our position and focus. The very thing we are trying to repel now becomes the God sent activity in our life. What I mean is, sometimes we fear losing our clients, and when we do eventually lose a client our heart can sink, we can worry and self destruct, but what happens is the client you thought was the sole life blood of your business actually isn't. In losing this client, it has given you the freedom to now work with two new clients whom you didn't have room for because the previous client took so much of your time and energy. What you once feared has now resulted in a world of opportunity and growth. Life is not to be feared but to be discovered. Sometimes, in order to regain focus and balance in our lives, our surroundings and beliefs need to be shaken up. In subsequent months after the issue with my physical balance, I learned the issue wasn't with my inner ear but my neck, I have had to work on my posture, exercise and stretch my neck muscles and make adjustments which trigger my neck from become misaligned. I had to change the way I operated sitting at a desk, taking time out to rest and listen to my body, strengthening my core. What an incredible metaphor when it comes to balance, we must change the way we do things in order to change the results and outcomes from our actions. If we never change our posture and the habits we have created in our life are misaligned, the world in which we live will seem skewed. To avoid this, we must journal our thoughts, observe the way we respond to activities, strengthen who we are and our value system, and we must sit up straight with integrity at the core of our being.

CHAPTER 10

Self Discovery

Turn yourself loose.

The film *Seabiscuit* is about a race horse sired by the legendary Hardtack and expected to follow in his father's footsteps. The Bay colt grew up on Claiborne Farm in Kentucky, where he was trained. He was undersized, knobby-kneed and given to sleeping and eating for long periods of time. Because of this, Seabiscuit was relegated to a punishing schedule of smaller races where he failed to win in his first 17. He was subsequently sold for a rock bottom price before finally being purchased by Charles Howard and trained by Tom Smith who used unorthodox training methods to bring Seabiscuit out of his lethargy. Improvements came quickly under the guidance of this team, and in their remaining eight races in the East, Seabiscuit and new jockey Red Pollard won several times.

In early November 1936, Howard and Smith shipped the horse to California by rail. His last two races of the year were at Bay Meadows racetrack in San Mateo, California. The first was the one-mile Bay Bridge Handicap. Despite starting badly and weighing in at 116 pounds (a top weight by racing standards), Seabiscuit won by five lengths. At the World's Fair Handicap (Bay Meadows' most prestigious stakes race), Seabiscuit led throughout.

The next year, in 1937, Seabiscuit battled with fellow contender Rosemont throughout the season with at least one loss widely attributed in the press to a jockey error. Pollard, who hadn't seen Rosemont over his shoulder until it was too late, was blind in one eye due to an accident during a training ride. Until this time, he'd managed to hide that fact throughout his career.

During this time, Seabiscuit rapidly was becoming a favourite among California racing fans, and his fame spread as he began a winning streak. With his success, Howard decided to ship the horse east for its more prestigious racing circuit. Seabiscuit's run of victories continued unabated. Between June 26 and August 7, he ran five times at stake's races, and each time he won despite steadily increasing handicap weights of up to 130 pounds. On September 11, Smith accepted an impost of 132 pounds for the Narragansett Special at Narragansett Park. On race day, the ground was slow and heavy and entirely unsuited to "the Biscuit." Smith wished to scratch, but Howard overruled him. Never in the running, had Seabiscuit trudged home in third place. His streak was snapped, but the season was not over. Seabiscuit won his next three races (one a dead heat) before finishing the year with a second place at Pimlico. That year, Seabiscuit won 11 of his 15 races and was the year's leading money winner in the United States. War Admiral, having won the Triple Crown that season, was voted the most prestigious honour, the American Horse of the Year Award.

In 1938, as a five-year-old, Seabiscuit's success continued. On February 19, Pollard suffered a terrible fall while racing on Fair Knightess, another of Howard's horses. With Pollard's chest crushed by the weight of the fallen horse, and his ribs and arm broken, Howard had to find a new jockey. After trying three, he settled on George Woolf, an already successful rider and old friend of Pollard, to ride Seabiscuit. Woolf's first race was the Santa Anita Handicap, the "hundred grander" Seabiscuit had narrowly lost the previous year. Seabiscuit was drawn on the outside and from the start was impeded by another horse, Count Atlas, angling out. The two were locked together for the first straight, and by the time Woolf had his horse disentangled, they were six lengths from the pace. The pair battled hard but was beaten in a photo finish by the fast finishing Santa Anita Derby winner, Stagehand.

After increasing success, the media began speculating about a match race between Seabiscuit and the seemingly invincible War Admiral. The two horses were scheduled to meet in three stakes races, but one or the other was scratched each time. By June, Pollard had recovered and agreed to work a young colt named Modern Youth. Spooked by something on the track, the horse broke rapidly through the stables and threw Pollard, shattering his leg and seemingly ending his career.

Meanwhile, Howard arranged a match race for Seabiscuit against the highly regarded Ligaroti. With Woolf once again aboard, Seabiscuit won the race despite persistent fouling from Ligaroti's jockey. After three more outings, and with only one win, he was scheduled to go head-to-head with War Admiral in the Pimlico Special in November. Dubbed, The Match of the Century, the event was jammed solid with fans. Trains brought fans from all over the country, and the estimated 40,000 at the track were joined by some 40 million listening on the radio. War Admiral was the favorite by a nearly unanimous selection of journalists and tipsters.

Head-to-head races favour fast starters, and War Admiral's speed from the gate was well known. Seabiscuit, on the other hand, was a pace stalker, skilled at holding with the pack before pulling ahead with late acceleration. From the scheduled walk-up start, few gave him a chance to lead War Admiral into the first turn. Smith knew these things, and had been secretly training Seabiscuit to run against this hype, using a starting bell and a whip to give the horse a burst of speed from the start.

When the bell rang, Seabiscuit ran away from the Triple Crown champion. Despite being drawn on the outside, Woolf led by over a length after just 20 seconds and soon crossed over to the rail position. Halfway down the backstretch, War Admiral started to cut into the lead, gradually pulling level with Seabiscuit, then slightly ahead. Following advice he had received from Pollard, Woolf had eased up on Seabiscuit, allowing his horse to see his rival before asking for more effort. Two hundred yards from the wire, Seabiscuit pulled away again and continued to extend his lead over the closing stretch, finally winning by four clear lengths despite War Admiral running his best time ever for the distance.

As a result of his races that year and the victory over War Admiral, Seabiscuit was named the 1938 American Horse of the Year, and he was the number one newsmaker that year. The only major prize that eluded him was the Santa Anita Handicap.

Seabiscuit had the DNA of a champion but wasn't initially in the appropriate environment to get the best out of him. It wasn't until Howard and Smith nurtured and understood him that he was able to succeed. Like Seabiscuit, the environment you create for yourself (or don't) will alter your results and create success. If the entrepreneurial gene is buried deep within you, it needs an opportunity to express itself. People can write you off and compare you to others (even family members), but it doesn't matter. Until you centre yourself, accept who you are and rediscover what you were born to do, you'll feel like you've come in second place, never reaching your potential. When you discover yourself, you'll find your purpose is in your passion.

CHAPTER 11

Authenticity

We are all a work in progress.

Remember when we talked about your competition not being against the people around you but against yourself? Nowhere is this more true than when you embrace authenticity. When you are your authentic self, you give yourself an open door to increase your influence. Look at your skills, find your inner sniper and elevate your unique selling point through your marketing and storytelling. Finding your inner sniper is about finding the right environment and culture that creates the right conditions for you to tap into the fullness of your being and execute with clarity and distinction your purpose and relevance— for yourself and your community. The most highly decorated Olympian, Michael Phelps, is a prime example of finding your inner sniper. His inner sniper is in the shape of a swimming pool, Michael comes alive, guns blazing, terrorising the competition because he's found an environment that harnesses and fuels his potential. The challenge for you and me is to find our own swimming pool to create the right conditions to create an explosion of excitement and purpose that will drive us forward and launch a tirade of passion and purpose within the context of our lives. Like Michael Phelps, become a scarce resource. When this is a focal point of who you are, your product or service will shine and people will come to you because you offer a solution to a very real problem. Creating your niche opens the door to influence and allows you to take your place within the market. Increased influence gives you the authority to blaze a new trail, liberate yourself from the mundane and evolve a new way of doing or experiencing things.

As a personal mentor to entrepreneurs, I've come to see the value in being real with my clients. If you stab a piece of sharp glass into my arm, I'll bleed. In order for people to trust you and accept your influence in their lives, they need to know you'll bleed. It means you're human. To accomplish this, I often share a current issue with which I'm dealing or reveal an area in my life where I may lack success or focus. I consistently find this level of sharing, rather than freak them out and have them thinking, "Why am I paying this clown to mentor me when he doesn't have it together!" actually articulates to them that we are all a work in progress. Life is a test. I'm authentically in tune with their problems, as well as my own, but I refuse to stay stuck where I am. I either learn to overcome or I hire someone who can perform where I may be lacking.

Being real and vulnerable doesn't mean you're weak but, instead, in touch with your most authentic self. People who embody authenticity are easier to trust and to take advice from. Trust is a key indicator of influence. We prefer to say "Yes" to those we know, like and trust. One way to gain trust is to share information about ourselves that shows our similarities and increases rapport. Maybe we have common goals or similar purposes? If you have people who work for you, equip them, give them ownership, credit them with success and give them a piece of the action. The way to influence others is to be the first to give, be responsible, exemplify an attitude of character and integrity, and be the prime communicator within your industry. If you don't have people who work for you, what about the people you live with or the team you are a part of? Authenticity will always lead to trust, and trust will lead to influence.

CHAPTER 12

Vitality

The opposite of depression is vitality.

For the past year, I've produced and shared a weekly YouTube video intended to inspire and educate. Receiving positive comments and community engagement reminds me why I take so much time to plan and record these videos. Nothing blesses me more than receiving a comment or private message noting how a video gave someone courage, insight, motivation or inspiration.

Now that some time has passed, subscribers have started asking me to cover specific topics. Most recently, I was asked to cover the subject of depression and dealing with negative thoughts. Depression is a deep subject and extremely complex. For that reason, I didn't want my message on the subject to be, "Pull your socks up, and get on with it." There are varying degrees of depression— some are clinical, others chemical and others environmental. However, I like to accept a challenge when someone who has been encouraged by my videos asks me to share.

As I began to focus on my own life and my goal to maintain a strong mental attitude and mindset, I re-evaluated my own key behaviours and actions that enable me to fight off feelings of depression, and a couple of behaviours spring to mind immediately. I have already mentioned the power of gratitude. It is such a powerful exercise. As with gratitude, something that has worked for me when feelings of depression creep in is to focus on the opposite of depression, which I believe to be vitality. When you focus on what you have, rather than what you don't, you create a life of abundance. Similarly when you focus on vitality, that zest, drive, fire and pep in your life, you begin to drive negative thoughts of depression away. I am mindful there are varying degrees of depression so I am not suggesting a few simple mindset shifts will solve the problem of clinical depression. The negative thoughts I'm speaking of are those common to all men. Studies have shown far too many people rest their minds in areas of sorrow, self pity and pain. It's often easier to say something than to do it, but negative self talk is self defeating, which is why sometimes you just need to tell that negative inner voice to shut up, and then take action instead.

Did you know you have the power to minister to yourself? Just as you can speak curses over your life, you can also speak blessings. The way you think of yourself, the conversations you have with yourself, affect the outcome of your life. Positive self talk is critical to pave the way for you to walk into your destiny and create a life of vitality and vibrancy. You must fill all your available head space with vitality, abundance and gratitude to starve negative, dark thoughts.

We all must be ruthless with whom we associate ourselves because we are the collective representation of the five people with whom we spend the most time— and you're one of them. Whom you allow to speak into your life is a key indicator of how much you respect yourself or, in some cases, how little. It's time to take action, rid yourself of those who are a negative influence in your life. If it's a family member who is not cultivating positivity in your life, limit your interaction with them. Life is challenging enough without having a dream killer in your inner circle.

Each month, I make conscious decisions with whom I need to limit my time and with whom I need to increase my time. I want to run with people who are fully charged— not perfect but positive. They have drive, they don't take "no" for an answer, they get knocked down and get straight back up and keep fighting. I like to call them "history makers" because they're ready to change the current of this world and leave their mark through being a person of influence.

One element to vitality that may not be immediately obvious is forgiveness. Forgiveness is for your benefit, not the person who did you wrong. When you choose not to forgive, you allow memories to imprison you and prevent you from moving forward in life. We've all been a victim at some point in our lives to varying degrees. Some of you may have faced awful inhumane situations. My call to you is you've already been hurt enough without allowing the past to imprison you, chain you up, stifle your relationships and stunt your success. Don't give the people in your past who did you wrong the satisfaction. Release them, forgive them, cut them out of your heart. It's supposed to be painful and difficult to forgive, but I encourage you to take the high road to find yourself restored and free. For others, it's the need to forgive yourself. Far too many people in the world are carrying huge burdens of guilt, shame and regret on their shoulders. Some people have been shouldering it so long it's almost become a part of their identity. Carrying this around is killing you, but you're blindsided by it and not thinking straight.

For people of faith, I'll share the story of King David, which always encourages me. God refers to David "as a man after my own heart," but David committed adultery and murdered the man whose wife he slept with to hide his mistakes. King David had enjoyed power and influence and often took advantage of situations. He did something wrong and was punished, but he carried on, asked for forgiveness and forgave himself. Before you turn the page to the next chapter, take a cue from King David and forgive yourself. We all fall short. We have all make mistakes— me included. Every day I make a mistake, and I forgive myself and ask for forgiveness. This process keeps my mind clear and strengthens my vitality. Life is for living— not holding onto shame and guilt. Our only obligation is to learn from mistakes, grow in maturity and kick on.

CHAPTER 13

Fear

Turn adversity into advantage.

Oh fear, that ugly, deceitful and cunning adversary that catches you unaware. It lurks in the shadows and waits to ambush you when you least expect it. It is subtle, and its purpose is to drive you off course, distract you from your dreams, throw curve balls, threaten you and push you back. It likes to hound, constrict and intimidate. Fear comes to your door when you are treading new ground, pushing boundaries and advancing. You're asking questions and being curious. Far too often, we make decisions on the back of fear pursuing us— the unknown, the what if. Fear is suggestive, and it will consume you if you let it. So, how do you combat fear? By dressing yourself in love.

My faith in Jesus and God is at the epicentre of all I am. When you do what you love, when you make decisions based on love, when you allow love to speak to you, awaken you and bring you peace, it drives fear away. It's important to centre yourself. When we're afraid, the temptation is to run. You see this during wild animal attacks. When you run, it only ignites the beast to pursue you. It's the same with fear, so look it in the eye. Stand your ground, centre yourself, reach out for help, go to your sanctuary, breathe and settle yourself. If you pray then pray, if you sing then sing. Focus on facts rather than suggestions or possibilities. Then, before making any decision, ask yourself what is driving you. If it's fear, hold off before committing to anything.

I'm not suggesting not to try to overcome your fear of heights or spiders. I'm talking about making decisions based on fear that will hold you back from your potential. Stop asking yourself questions like, "What happens if I fail?" "What if I marry the wrong person?" "What happens if my business doesn't work?" "What happens if I get sick and can't fulfill the life I want?" Asking those questions from a place of fear stops you in your tracks. You'll never leave the confines of your house. You'll never make new friends. You'll never start a business, and you'll walk around in a quarantine outfit to prevent sickness. We can't live like that.

That's what terrorism does. It puts up barriers in our minds that paralyse us and prevent us from moving forward. I know people who won't leave their own country because they're afraid of terrorism. I know people who won't set up a business because of the debt they may get into. In life, anything is possible and anything can happen if you're doing what you love. If you allow love and passion to drive you, you may hit up against fear from time to time but it won't overwhelm you. Don't give fear the satisfaction. Fight it, resist it, smile at it, sing at it and push it back come hell or high water. I shall advance, I shall not let fear be my Commander in Chief, I shall not be bound in fear. In my case, I have faith in Jesus Christ to be the lifter of my head, my strong tower, my fortress and shield. Whatever you see as your castle, high ground and sanctuary, settle there before making decisions you may regret if made from a place of fear.

Fear isn't the only adversary in life. We all face setbacks and obstacles because adversity rears its head in numerous forms. It seems the world is full of people going through extreme adversity both personally and professionally. You can't always control your circumstances, but you can control how you choose to respond. It's time to turn your adversity into your advantage. When something unexpected hits you between the eyes and you weren't aware of the possible danger, it leaves you stunned. It knocks you off balance, and stops you in your tracks. Some never recover from adversity but, if you have the right mindset and are prepared, adversity is a huge opportunity for self discovery.

Often our fondest and most cherished moments are on the back of overcoming the odds, being the underdog, facing extreme conditions and unlikely outcomes. Life will throw you some curve balls and some threats. Be aware of your adversary, but don't be afraid. You can't show your strength if you have nothing and nobody to overcome. Adversity gives you the power and opportunity to flex your muscles, to keep you resourceful and flexible. Do you have the courage to stand your ground even when everyone else around you is backing down? Are you resolute? Contrite? Fortified? When you're backed into a corner, how do you respond? Do you let life beat on you, manipulate you and overcome you? Or do you centre yourself, seek a way out, grow bigger than your problems and fight back?

My parent's divorce was an adversary. As Samuel Lover famously said, "Circumstances are the rulers of the weak; But, they are the instruments of the wise." When I've not seen the road ahead, I've often realised it's time to fly. The road to success isn't always a road. When you embrace a victim mentality, there is no growth. You go through suffering and pain, becoming disempowered and suffer without ever learning the lesson hidden there. Turning your adversity into your advantage is about shifting your mindset from victim to victor. We all have battle wounds. It's time to take those scars and turn them into pearls of wisdom. These wounds leverage and project you forward to inspire courage for others— and for yourself.

If you're in a battle right now in your relationships, health or business, it's time to look it in the eye, centre yourself, ask for help if you need to and find the positivity to move forward. Sometimes, all you can do is stand your ground and tell adversity it's met its match. You'll probably surprise yourself. You were made to overcome.

Overcoming external adversity can sometimes seem far more simple than overcoming the internal variety. It's human nature to self sabotage, and the temptation is always there. Sometimes we get stuck in unhealthy behaviours and thoughts. It can appear in the form of addictions or can be the result of unhealthy beliefs about ourselves. It can be rooted in shame and guilt. Often an emotional experience or setback can take a stronghold in our mind, and that constantly shuts us down.

I recently suffered a problem with my iPad. Each time the iPad fired up, the Apple logo flashed briefly before the machine died instantly. This went on for days. I searched the Web, spoke to contacts and tried every piece of advice I came across. Sometimes, you have to exhaust all your options before you realise you don't always have all the answers. I scheduled a slot at a local Apple store, and two hours later my iPad had been reprogrammed and was back up and running. Sometimes we need to be reprogrammed to get back up and running. The difficult bit about self sabotage is that we often recognize a problem but are unwilling to make a change or unaware of where to get help. You find yourself in a cycle. You make progress and are fired up, but each time it is an endless cycle until, eventually, this limiting belief or addiction gets the better of you and shuts you down.

When it comes to self-sabotage, procrastination is king. Why? Because procrastination is the gap between intention and action, and it is in this gap that the self operates. The undermining behaviour lies in not closing the gap. We intend to act but, when the time comes, we get lost in deliberation and make excuses to justify a potentially harmful delay to action. We must put a stop to it. We must daily reflect and take action. We must break the common triggers and thought processes that encourage us to ignore our own creativity and spirit. Take time to observe yourself. Journal these observations. Remind yourself that success isn't defined by a silver bullet. Success varies in all its forms. Don't throw the baby out with the bath water. Life doesn't have to be perfect. Seek progression and not perfection.

CHAPTER 14

Failure

*I've learned so much from my mistakes
that I've decided to make more.*

"Ever tried? Ever failed? No matter. Try again, fail again and fail better." These were the words of Irish playwright Sam Beckett. Unless we're willing to leave the comfort of our armchair, take risks and fail, we can't lead a life of advancement and leadership. Leadership starts with you, and you can't really lead if you don't love. Loving yourself is the first step to great leadership. This isn't about thinking you're better than anyone else but about the ability to be a fabulous steward of your mind, body and spirit. When we lead out of love, it allows us to express ourselves, to reach out and explore life and all its opportunities and offerings. When we express, test, explore and examine new thoughts or ways of doing things, we will fail— we will slip up. Beckett was encouraging his readers that it doesn't matter if we fail. What really matters is that we try, that we don't give up, that we evolve and reinvent ourselves. Challenging the status quo and bringing a new paradigm to the way we think and operate turns failure into success.

Often, we're unaware when we are failing. It takes courage and maturity to examine the decisions and choices we make every day, and self reflection is a key component to this process. Constantly evaluating your mental GPS and being mindful of the current struggle will help you fail better. If I'd learned to fail more often and more quickly, the lessons I've now learned would have come to me significantly faster. When we learn, we grow. So, why resist staying comfortable? Why not test the boundaries, stir up the curiosity and fail better?

It takes more courage to examine your soul than it does for a soldier to take to the battlefields. With that in mind, I dare to say very few people take time to look into their own soul because they're gripped by fear of the shame, guilt and mistakes laden through their lives. This fear prevents us from journeying through our own wounds, disappointments and setbacks. The most painful journeys are the ones that go through your heart, but they're also the most valuable, exciting and ground breaking.

Preparing your heart, mind and understanding to allow new revelations and thoughts to come to the fore will encourage and entice success within your life. The need to be prepared is of vital importance to grow and advance. As mentioned earlier, "When opportunity comes, it's too late to prepare." This is so true. When we're not reflective and looking within our soul, we're not prepared for the good, bad and ugly that most certainly will arise during the course of our life. However, when we're conscious of our own life and what's going on in our soul, we're set to take the learning and failings and draw the positives out of both to make us stronger, wiser and battle ready.

Babe Ruth said, "Every strike out gets me closer to the home run." You have to be in the game to win. You have to come out swinging. Sure, there will be times you'll miss or strike out but, as you expose yourself to the challenge, it increases your skill and knowledge. The key to success is having faith that opportunities will keep coming— life will keep throwing you a ball. You can leave the field, you can allow the ball to hit you or pass you by, or you can develop a strategy, mindset and principle to connect with the ball and hit a home run. Too often we focus on the problem and not the solution. Stop allowing life to pass you by because a few of the balls thrown at you have hit you in the eye. Reposition yourself, improve your vision and get smart. I've learned so much from my mistakes that I've decided to make some more.

CHAPTER 15

Setbacks

*The only people who don't get flat tyres
are those who don't drive.*

The road to failure often is laden with setbacks. This morning, a Monday, I headed out to my car and instantly saw a flat tyre. When Mondays are so valuable to you and you use them to create the head space you need in order to set up your week, these sorts of delays come as a blow. Today is a great story of how setbacks can knock us off track, hinder and obstruct our day, but still provide us the opportunity to make a choice. We can get mad, become frustrated and maybe even throw ourselves a pity party, or we can resolve ourselves that setbacks are just a part of life. Things happen that we least expect, but that doesn't mean it's time to lose your head. Instead, it's the perfect time to steady yourself and find a resolution to the latest obstacle.

My obstacle this morning was a flat tyre. Was it a hindrance? Absolutely. But, some things just aren't worth stealing your peace over even if that means you have to work a little harder and longer today. Life doesn't always go according to plan. It's right to have an agenda— rule your day or the day will rule you— but your agenda should be viewed as a roadmap that may occasionally have detours. Let me go a little deeper with the flat tyre. I had a puncture because I was driving on dirty roads covered in glass, screws and nails. The only people who don't get flat tyres are those who don't drive, and those who don't experience setbacks are not living out of their comfort zone. These people are living in a bubble, rarely venturing from the comfort of their home or office.

Setbacks occur when you're on a journey, advancing and experiencing new terrain. If you want an easy life, if you like to be comfortable but never grow, if you want to put up walls around your heart because of the fear of pain, be my guest. But, that mindset isn't an option in my life, and I suggest you eradicate it from your life if you want to succeed. We were born to advance, to explore and drive. Pain, problems, obstacles and setbacks will come. In fact, our journey may grind to a complete halt, but when you have to be somewhere, when you have a place to go, you can't give up. Fix the problem, or find someone who can.

What should have taken ten minutes to remove the tyre took me an hour. I had a problem with the jack to start with. It kept slipping from under my car. Then, I couldn't get enough leverage to undo the bolts and wheel nuts. Once I had removed the nuts off my tyre, it was clamped shut to the wheel arch, and I needed three bricks to stop the car from rolling. That was hard work for a punctured tyre. I easily could have become vexed and, at times, I could feel the frustration creeping in. Looking at the clock didn't help my cause. Thankfully a neighbour offered some assistance, which I gladly accepted. We all need to be mindful of when to accept help. Being unable to solve a problem by yourself is not a sign of weakness. We're not to play God in our lives but to be faithful with the skills and strengths we're given while appreciating the skills and strengths of others.

We're relational beings and must understand the importance of surrounding ourselves with people who are better than us. This way, whatever the setback and challenge, we can be encouraged because this setback is a result of your positive activity to advance and take new ground. You've not settled for the easy road or, worse still, not taken the road at all choosing instead to stay in the comfort of your home. Understand when to ask for help, be resourceful, stop focusing on the problem and look for solutions. If a solution doesn't easily come to you, ask people who are specialists in your area of challenge for help. Most importantly, don't lose hope or focus. You'll be back on the road before long.

CHAPTER 16

Diversion

It is vital we pay attention to our own mental GPS.

Late last night, as I was walking an associate back to her car, the car park was closed and we were unable to get her car out. We phoned the management and asked if the car park could be opened. The answer was not until 7am. Since it was already late in the evening and my associate lives 30 miles away, I suggested I take her home and for her to catch a train the next day to collect her car. In the end, I drove half way and my associate was collected by one of her friends. Problem solved— or so I thought. Had I keyed in the coordinates to return home on my GPS, I would have found that the motorway I've taken lots of times before was closed and my GPS would have re-calibrated my journey. But, on this occasion mile after mile it was telling me to turn around. I must have travelled five miles knowing I was going in the wrong direction hoping and praying it would take me on an alternative route. There is nothing more soul destroying than knowing you're going the wrong way. Taking a different route, not having all the answers, gives rise to panic and uncertainty when all you really want to do is get home. On this occasion, I had to trust that the GPS system was going to pick up a trail and take me home. I won't lie. I did feel a little challenged by the experience, heading down dark, muddy roads in the rain. I had to hit on the brakes a number of times and didn't feel I was progressing, but I trusted this tiny little piece of machinery knew better than I did. Had it been a beautiful, sunny day, it would have been a glorious experience, but the conditions and the dark torrential downpour were far from ideal.

It is vital we know and trust our own mental GPS. The framework of my mentoring relationship with entrepreneurs is based on a GPS system featuring eight key fundamentals that make up a person's basic DNA. Through this system, blind spots are revealed alongside efficiencies and deficiencies. We have to learn how to centre ourselves, and understand that whatever comes at us in life, we listen to our inner voice and compass— even if it seems backward, confusing and full of uncertainty. Diversions come our way in different forms. I could have pulled into a hotel or a pub and asked for help or stayed overnight somewhere until I knew the motorway was open the following morning or I could problem solve, try alternative routes and not give up. When it comes to thoughts, suggestions and even temptations, knowing which way to go is far simpler when you have a centre point.

To get your bearings is critical. If home is your goal, you just have to do what you have to do in order to arrive at your destination. Life is like that, but many people are pulled over on the side of the road paralysed by the unknown. While I didn't enjoy the journey and the inconvenience, it spoke to me and strengthened my mind. Life is full of road blocks and diversions— circumstances change, economics change, relationships change, people say, "No." You may have had success in one area and may have thought you had it all figured out just when life threw you a curve ball. If you've dropped the ball, it's time to pick it up again and head for home.

CHAPTER 17

Success

Success is about being at peace with yourself.

We all want to be successful, but what defines success is different for different people. I remember going out into my local town to interview people about what success meant to them for a local radio station. It was clear that for many material possessions or a nice house, car and financial stability were ranked very highly in their quest for personal success. For others, it was their health or strength of relationship with family and friends. Success is formed in different ways, and what success means to you is a great question to ask when considering a life full of purpose. If you don't distinguish what success means for you, how will you know when you've achieved it?

Success for me is a journey— not a destination. Success is constantly moving, but it's an internal accomplishment rather than an external one. I've worked with millionaires who are miserable and unhappy, and I've worked with those who own startup businesses with very little money but who find themselves motivated and full of zest for life. Success is about being at peace with yourself. Can you look in the mirror and know you're playing to your strengths by being authentic and true to yourself? Are you living a life of integrity?

During a recent talk at a local college, a student actually asked if I was at peace with myself. Now, that's a great question! After defining what I believed to be success in my life, I began searching deep inside myself and realised I had been rather smug that I knew what success was, but I wasn't as confident to say I was at peace with myself. Each of us is our own worst critic. I'm a work in progress and so are you. We're all struggling with internal battles, confusion and tension, but this is often a result of advancement. Sometimes earthquakes happen due to friction from one position to the next, but I would rather have a life full of movement and risk the earthquake than live a safe and stagnant life.

There are a number of ways to cultivate an environment that enables success to flourish and embrace being at peace with yourself. You must learn to dream. Once you've allowed yourself to dream, you must start to live it, breathe it and allow it to consume you. You can often find your dream when you take time out to rest and allow your mind to come alive. It's crucial you don't just have great thoughts and great dreams— you must then fuel them with action.

You must continue to believe in your ideas and be the best you can be. There's no point in doing anything you don't truly believe and have resolute confidence in. If you don't believe in your product or service, your potential customers won't either and this could harm your personal brand and certainly your business. Continually seek out and revaluate what you are passionate about and how you can introduce it into your business to impact and improve your customer experience.

Life gets so serious at times and a big part of being successful is having fun. It shows great character to be able to continue laughing even in the face of adversity. Often, when I'm feeling blue, I up the amount of dance parties I schedule into my day. A dance party is when I find a favourite music track and spend a few minutes just getting my groove on. I shake my body, get in the zone and shake off that sense of trouble, failure and struggle. The temptation is always to give up when you feel overwhelmed. Time and again, you hear that at just the point when you're about to throw in the towel, your breakthrough comes. Be steadfast. When the wind blows and the waves crash, stand your ground, lift your head, straighten your shoulders, take some deep breaths and revaluate. Your breakthrough may be just over the horizon. Being an entrepreneur is very much an adventure. Whatever comes your way, look it in the eye and don't forget what your purpose is.

We were made to explore, to be curious. The ability and responsibility to set yourself new challenges keeps you moving forward. Too often, yesterday's success comes at the expense of today because we allow it to fuel our ego rather than appreciating the journey is not yet complete. In Formula One racing, they have a pre-match event to determine where a driver will feature on the grid. This is determined by how quickly they can complete the course, and drivers are then placed in order of rank based on their times. It's no good celebrating being first on the grid if you haven't faced the real race yet. Don't become sidelined and allow success to go to your head. There is still plenty in front of you, and you don't want to miss it.

At the start of the book, I shared my childhood and the difficulties I faced in my relationships. While we're busy creating a personal revolution, we mustn't lose track of our family. Relationships are the one area you can't ignore. It's not healthy to be alone for long periods of time. Introvert or not, we all need to connect and be involved in stimulating conversations. The importance of delegation in your professional life enables you to protect your time with family and friends. The key, as with so much in life, is finding balance. That's why my focus isn't the nice house or the nice car. I could end up living and driving on my own because I traded material success for the success of my family and friends.

To ensure I spend quality time with my family and friends, I limit the amount of television I watch. I do enjoy watching movies; However, there is a time when we just need to unplug and get outside. Go and explore. Be adventurous. Sundays in my home are called "Sephton Sundays." We do something together as a family— go for a walk, play a game, find something that doesn't just involve watching the T.V. Often, that takes some planning. It doesn't need to be a Sunday, but I recommend finding a day where you venture beyond the comforts of home, and take your family with you.

One personal motivation that leads to a bounty of success in my life is found in the unlikeliest of places. When people speak badly of me, my product or service, I take this as a challenge because it provides a fabulous motivator to prove them wrong. It's the same when people write you off or play down the potential of your ideas and actions. Why do people love to see others suffer and have setbacks? Yet, so many do. The onslaught they fire at you needs to serve as motivation that you are getting out there, hustling and making a stand. Stand for something, or fall for everything. I believe when you do what you love and are sold out for your business and, most importantly, your vision and purpose you will have the last laugh because your life will be a parade of success and virtue. Remember to define what success is to you. These thoughts I share will help you get there and, remember, insults are wonderful motivators.

How to Create a Life of Success

- Celebrate somebody else's achievements
- Believe in your ideas
- Invest in the areas where you're already influential
- Have regular dance parties to take 3 minutes out of your day and groove to your favourite song
- Be Positive! It breeds opportunity
- Love people, and build an organic community
- Give— without expectation of something in return
- Have a hunger for personal development
- Have a servant's heart: Stop selling and teach them how to buy
- Follow your gut
- Live out of your personal brand
- Take risks
- Stop complaining, and turn your whining into winning
- Embrace a lifestyle of grit and a resolute mentality to progress

Once you've defined what success is to you, create a framework, a battle plan if you will, and get to work. Life is a journey, not a destination. Success can't be defined by someone else. It's you and you alone who will determine if you've lived a successful life. Embrace and cultivate some of the action points above to really stimulate a positive flow of success. Be rich in your giving because others benefit and depend on your success too. Remember, being the best you can be really can change the world in which we live and make a difference in the lives of others. It's crucial you make a difference in the lives of others. Through your life and your business, it's paramount that who and what you are influences others in a way that makes them fly. When you truly make a difference to how someone feels, you will not be forgotten, and you create the wind they need to soar.

"To whom much is given, much is required."
–Luke 12:48 (ESV)

CHAPTER 18

Heart

"I've learned that people will forget what you said, people will forget what you did, but people will never forget how you made them feel." – Maya Angelou

Whatever you let into your heart has the ability to zap your strength. Consider Samson in the Bible. His strength came from his hair, so his strength quickly evaporated when his hair was cut. He had given his heart to his hair. When his hair was cut, he surrendered his power. Be mindful of what and to whom you give your heart and energy. If your heart and energy are given to the right people and endeavours, you can create a life of vitality, strength and courage. Protect your heart above all else because in your heart is where the rivers of your dreams, soul, destiny, and purpose pool. Whatever you're investing in, whether it is time, money or emotion, make sure it's nurturing you to be better.

More and more people are suffering physically due to emotional burnout and stress. We are all relational. We were created to relate and form relationships to comfort, challenge and build. Life, and its relationships, can be the most amazing privilege if they're positive experiences, but many are not. People find themselves in bad relationships, settling for second best, trying to make a point, continually looking for validation and selling their souls to be accepted. Some are in abusive relationships and suffer daily. But, the biggest devastation to the heart is in those who think everything is okay but are living a life of delusion where everything looks amazing on the outside but on the inside is cold, dark and empty.

Take back control and ownership of your hearts. Have wisdom around to whom you reveal your inner self. See your heart as the most precious commodity you possess. If you're tired, have a good look at the endeavours and people you're giving yourself to. You may need to make some immediate adjustments to restore the strength of your heart. Where your treasure is, your heart will be also. You can often see what you value by the time and energy you give to it. When you treasure something, you pour your all into it. This is a great indicator that what you value, you treasure and what you treasure is where your heart will be. Don't fall victim to being left empty because all you did was give. While it's very noble and throughout this book I'm banging the drum for you to give, you must know when your soul needs restoring. Taking time out, asking for help, having a soul sabbatical is all a part of the bigger picture to keep your heart strong and vibrant. Each of us can only give out of what we have. It doesn't serve you or your network in giving out the dregs of your heart. You owe it to yourself to be wise in the areas you invest. You cannot give your pearls to swine, and you can't empty yourself and be short changed. Look at the people and exercises that give you energy, people who help you rest and activities that restore your mind and soul. I regularly have a massage to release tension and to bring me to a place where I can refuel.

CHAPTER 19

Maxims

"If you don't change direction you end up where you are now." – Unknown

The values or maxims by which you live become a part of your own DNA, and they're paramount as you shift gears and become more mindful of which opportunities to seize and which to let pass you by. A maxim really is a rule of conduct by which you live and a personal barometer to measure your own rules of engagement. In my life, there are nine maxims I intentionally try to uphold.

We're all on a journey of self improvement and the pursuit of excellence. Some of my own rules of conduct have become second nature and others I consciously have to look at developing and nurturing. As you read this chapter, allow my maxims to pass a due diligence test in your own life. Feel free to adopt these into your life or edit as necessary. Search your heart and introduce your own maxims to create a personal framework by which to live.

1. Be Authentic

My first rule is to be my authentic self and to be real about my thoughts, feelings, frustrations, struggles and successes. The only person you hurt is yourself when you hide behind the opinion of others or behind other people's success. The liberating thing about being authentic is that nobody can compare you to someone else. We're all different, and that's something worth having a personal revelation around. I don't know anyone who is like me. Depending on your viewpoint, that could be either disappointing or a relief. Either way, to be assured and comfortable in your own skin takes time and often requires lots of positive self talk and a focus on leading others by confronting issues head-on rather than people pleasing. Former U.S. Secretary of State Colin Powell said, "Trying to get everyone to like you is a sign of mediocrity. You'll avoid the tough decisions, you'll avoid confronting people who need to be confronted, and you'll avoid offering different rewards based on different performance because some people may get upset." When you embrace your own authentic style, it won't be a question of people pleasing. Good leadership is not a popularity contest.

2. Be Grateful

My life is filled with gratitude. We all have a choice where we focus our attention. We can be empowered or disabled depending on our viewpoint, mindset and outlook. Gratitude produces a life of abundance. The word 'abundance' derives from the ocean, which is constant, free and overflowing with wave after wave hitting the shore. Having an abundant life is stimulated by a life of gratitude. We can all find things in our life to moan and grumble about, but that leads to a miserable, lonely life focusing on what is lacking and comparing yourself to others. It's far better to take the high road, look at what you have and focus on your strengths, talents, skills and relationships.

We're all supposed to be successful and your success and favour will increase when you focus on being appreciative. Each day before I sleep, I reflect and write at least three things for which I'm grateful. Sometimes we take certain factors for granted (like our health or the fact we can put food on the table). It's time to be grateful. I even know one person who went a step further and writes two thank you cards to two significant people in her life each month. What a fabulous gratitude practice.

3. Be Intentional

My next maxim is based on being intentional. We can't grow beyond our current state if we're not intentional about our personal growth plan. We must be dedicated to increasing our knowledge, wealth and understanding and then turn each concept into action. For example, I have a personal growth plan and a budget for personal growth. I set goals for the books I want read, the seminars I want to attend, and the mentoring I open myself up to. I know if I want to be bigger than my problems, I must be intentional at adapting, evolving and growing my mind and conditioning my sense of direction.

It is rare we grow outside of being intentional. On rare occasions a health scare or the death of a loved one or other extreme circumstances can launch us into radical changes that bring a level of growth. But, generally, being reactive rather than proactive leads only to frustration. To be intentional really means to have focus and a plan to execute. It's about aiming in the right direction. Certainly, being intentional doesn't exist in a vacuum, but it is the building block to ensure you're involved in the race. Once you have a focus and a blueprint of action, you must execute. If you don't have a plan to develop your skill, mind, relationships and business, then you need to sit down and decide to what and whom you need to expose yourself and in what to invest to take you to the next level. As an old proverb once said, "If you don't change direction, you end up where you are now."

4. Be a River

Once you're intentional and realise that gratitude leads to abundance, you're in a position to live my next maxim:
Be a river, not a reservoir. Who we are and what we have is not just for personal gain. Far too many people believe their success and wealth is only for themselves. While there is nothing wrong with having nice things, living in a big mansion and driving a flashy car, life should be about more. My challenge to you is this: Who are you going to buy a mansion for? What family are you going to bless with a new car?

Being a river and not a reservoir is about sharing your wealth, knowledge and skill. I encourage you to lay down the gauntlet of whom you can liberate and invest in to make a significant difference in their lives and those around them. Who can drink and feast from your success and abundance? Who can ride on the current of your wealth? Some may try to take advantage of you, so I'm not asking you to be unwise— only to realise that your success is bigger than you. Enjoy your life, and then go help a bunch of people enjoy their life too. Educating and mentoring those around you is so rewarding. Create a legacy of abundance, have a reputation for being a river of resource and value who gives freely rather than a reservoir that only holds success within its banks.

5. Invest in Yourself

My own personal development journey really began when I started to invest in myself. This is a key maxim to unlock doors in your life, and it's one I'm very conscious and intentional about. Most of the stories I've shared in this book sprung out of investing in myself: My attitude, character, outlook, relationships and skill set. We're all powerful beyond measure, and we have the ability to grow and move wherever we so choose. We are not trees planted by our roots. We can get up and change the course of our lives by our choices and actions.

Investing in yourself is both exciting and exhilarating. It's through our senses that we build an infrastructure of values which determine our outlook and confidence. It's what we see and look at that imprints an image in our mind. It's what we taste and like or dislike. It's what we feel and either acknowledge or run away from. Our senses are sensitive and powerful. Have you ever smelled something and it's taken you back to a long ago memory? Maybe a childhood holiday or romance? That's why it's imperative that what we allow our senses to be exposed to is both wise and in line with who we are. I'm encouraged by my own personal growth over the past six years, but I'm also aware there is lots more to come. I am a sponge when it comes to learning and cultivating my own knowledge, understanding and gifts. I put time and money into my own growth and continue to work my personal plan. When you improve you, you also improve your opportunities. That's why I love mentoring entrepreneurs so much. I don't exclusively focus on business or financial success. I focus on people: The mind, the thoughts and the attitude. That's where the key to success lies— not in doing more but in building your own inner sniper to harness your strengths and skills to blaze a trail and change your life through your authentic, incredible gifts.

Once you learn to invest in yourself, you'll find yourself empowered to invest in others. To effectively invest in others, we must first fully live out the power of investing in ourselves. When you go on an airplane, the cabin crew delivers the safety talk. One of the safety measures that is particularly relevant here is that of the oxygen masks that drop down from the overhead compartments when oxygen drops to an unsafe level. If you are travelling with children, the temptation in such an event is to help those around you before you help yourself. However, the guidelines of best practice encourage passengers to help themselves before reaching out to help others.

Investing in yourself first actually enables you to help others more effectively. If we mask ourselves with oxygen first, we can make better choices, stay calm and be responsible. When we help others before ourselves, we panic, make poor choices and, in extreme circumstances, self sabotage our performance and life. There's no point being a martyr when you could have been a hero.

The maxim to be a river and not a reservoir encourages us all to give of our skills and talents. If you have a team of people who work for you or you coach a little league team or even have children, you'll know the importance of investing in others. When done correctly, it not only improves your team, it also helps you, as efficiency and productivity increase and team morale reaches new heights. Investing in others also creates ample opportunities to create long-lasting legacies and relationships. I want people to speak highly of me for the way I led, inspired and motivated them, but I'm not going to obtain such an endorsement if I don't take the time to invest in others. Investment really is giving of your time, energy and resources to those who appreciate it. Remarkably, the more I invest in others, the more others have invested into me and the more happy and exciting surprises have come into my life. Some people are just looking for a little encouragement, time and attention. Think about who you can invest in. Who will most benefit and appreciate it? Leave a legacy by giving back to your community in some small way. Not only is it extremely rewarding, but I think you'll find the more you invest in others, the more you'll invest in yourself.

6. Expand Your Network

I'm a big believer in expanding your network and introducing yourself to different ideas and people. I'm not advocating becoming a serial networker, herded into a room like cattle, stand up, sit down, deliver a polished 60-second speech with no heart. The whole thing is a turn off. It's far better to connect at a heart level with someone and this isn't always best served in a networking group. Networking should be vibrant, relaxed and fluid. For example, many of the Tweet ups I've been to locally allow people to relate and get out of their own way, which in turn lets relationships form organically.

It's not enough to vaguely say, "I'm going to expand my network." Set a goal to meet two new people each week. When you organise a one-to-one meeting, you connect much more quickly and deeply with your new acquaintance. It's an investment of time and energy to understand a person's skills and what motivates them. When you carve out time to have some focused, uninterrupted time to develop a working relationship, you get to a place of authentic trust much more quickly.

If you've ever been on the receiving end of my persistent messages, Tweets, emails and texts, you'll know my communication is fueled by my desire to get to know you and invest in a relationship that serves us both. I like to meet with purpose because, when I understand what you do, I better understand how I can best help you obtain your dreams and aspirations. Last year I met with 112 new people and have established a strong connection with most of them. Some have become my clients and others I've become theirs. Sometimes, you make a connection and may not do anything together for years while you find yourself working together with others after just a few weeks.

I am extremely relational. I love people and my network is a point of pride for me because each one is valuable, different and unique. I challenge you to be the same. When you build a network, people naturally ask you if you know anyone in a particular field when they have that need. This is a great opportunity to create a win-win and be the go-to person in your community. It creates business for your contacts and credibility for you. Your wealth, like mine, isn't so we can become rich in a silo, but so we can leverage our own strengths and build a community. Do you take time to invest and nurture new relationships? If you don't, start now. I love meeting new people and am always ready to learn and to serve. Start each day with that mindset and people will naturally be positive about your introduction and help.

7. Practice Forgiveness

When a focus of your life is on relationships, it is inevitable that pain and disappointment comes at the hands of other human beings. Mistakes happen. People make choices that result in pain and hurt. Despite the inevitable, I'm completely sold on forgiveness. Forgiveness has always been, and will always be, for your benefit. When we choose not to forgive, we hold onto pain and anguish, and we actually allow the person who hurt us to imprison us and render us helpless. Not only does this result in building walls of protection that prevent you from moving forward with others, it also allows fear and pain to control your future and limit opportunities.

At times, we all fall victim to the desire to withhold forgiveness. This is more unhealthy than the pain you suffered at the hands of someone else. I've seen extreme breakthroughs with clients when they forgive those who have caused them pain. The power in releasing hurt from your heart and life has incredible results. More so, even, than you may imagine if you're currently wrestling with this concept. Like anything else in life, you have a choice to make. Forgiving the past frees you to optimize performance, get more restful sleep, spend more time with loved ones, make new connections and can even help you look and feel better.

The power of forgiveness is significant, and the results far outweigh the satisfaction of holding onto resentment. A word of warning: I'm not asking you to forget, as we need to take the learning from life lessons. If we, by our actions or choices, encouraged someone to cause us pain then we need to become more wise to limit or eradicate a situation that isn't healthy. It shows great wisdom to not open yourself up when hurt and pain is the inevitable result of an unwise decision. Allow your heart to be real and express itself. You owe yourself the courage to risk being hurt again. Just be mindful of whom you entrust in your life, whom you open up to, whom you allow to influence you and whom you allow to speak into your life. Some people don't deserve your time and attention. Be wise in your business and relationships, but don't let fear, pain and unforgiveness hold you back anymore.

8. Wear a Smile

In the film *Annie* I won't forget the words "You're never fully dressed without a smile." How true! That's my eighth maxim. A smile communicates a thousand words. A smile says you know who you are, and you know where you're heading. It gives you an air of confidence, trust and ease. A smile can light up a room, it can break the ice, and it can be warm, genuine and subtle. It's an action not bound by culture, language, race or religion. Everyone understands a smile. It's so positive it can change the mood, culture and demeanour of a person and situation.

Many know me as a super positive, enthusiastic individual. Joy is my strength, my weapon, my language. We've all heard how we'll have less wrinkles the more we smile because it gives your face a workout, but it's also a declaration of truth. Often when I've smiled upon my problems, setbacks and challenges, my mind begins buying into the idea that this difficulty soon will pass. By smiling, I'm setting up my mind and body for victory. Your situation may look bleak and, of course, there's a time to grieve and be sad depending on the circumstances, but we all have a choice. There is a song by Nat King Cole that sings, "Smile, though your heart is aching." This is a declaration that the good times will come— that this season of difficulty will pass.

Smiling is as beneficial to you as it is to those at whom you smile. I often think the most beautiful and attractive people are the ones who smile. It's the biggest weapon any sales person can have. Not words, but a smile. Do you have a life full of happy smiles? Do you get dressed with a smile? Sometimes, smiling is easier than others. I'm not asking you to fake it. I'm encouraging you to act and allow your feelings to follow and move into the framework of happiness and joy. People want to be around positive people. Smiling is contagious and infectious. It lifts the spirits, opens doors, blazes trails, blows open the window, puts a spring in your step and waves a banner of victory for all to see. A smile shows the world you're winning. Why are you not smiling more? It's good for your mental and physical health. Now is the time to smile.

9. Do Not Quit

My final maxim is do not quit. This message is like a beating drum. The more entrepreneurs I meet, the more I hear them bang the drum of not quitting. I'm encouraged the same message is always so strong and consistent. We often quit at the cusp of our breakthrough. We faint, throw in the towel and withdraw from our endeavours and adventures, but anything of value will always cost you something. Where is the value if it's just handed to you on a plate? I like competition, and I like a challenge because you have to evolve, be resourceful and think outside the box. You have to grow and develop. You have to be quicker, stronger and wiser. That takes time, investment and dedication.

When we consider our why, the reason we get out of bed, our life's purpose, our vision and mandate, it's very hard to quit when your why becomes bigger than your will or how. We may not have all the answers, but we know where we're heading and we remain resolute until we cross the finish line. Will power isn't enough. Why power is what we must stir up within ourselves to remain firmly planted on the goal rather than distracted by what life throws at us. Blood, sweat and tears will not deter our need to overcome, so be true to yourself. Do not quit, do not faint, do not buy other people's stories. Don't make excuses, listen to your heart, encourage yourself. Replay past achievements, and reflect on the struggles and the fights you've already overcome. Be encouraged by how you stood your ground. Your past should spur you on, encourage you and vanquish your fears and doubts. You can achieve greatness! You are powerful beyond all measure! You can change the course of your life! You can make a difference and be a positive influence in your community! You can be known as someone who is relentless and persistent, who doesn't take no for an answer, who pushes the boundaries and changes the environment in which you dwell. You can do it! Minister to yourself, speak well of yourself, be positive, write and read personal affirmations, surround yourself with people who overcame the odds. It will all help you develop an attitude that quitting is not an option.

CHAPTER 20

Law of Attraction

Google it, research it, picture it and live it.

Through the course of my work, I talk with many people about the law of attraction. During these talks, I've found again and again that if you have an expectation to seize opportunities and create a mindset like that of a fisherman who expects a great catch, sooner or later you'll find yourself reeling in the catch of your life. Having a mindset that nurtures opportunities, blessings and successes, I know first hand this is true.

A great example of the law of attraction is your dream car. You Google it, you research it, you read its specs and performance capabilities, you create a mental picture and may even take it a step further and download a photo onto your computer. You go visit a local dealership and may even take it for a test drive. Your dream is starting to feel more tangible. As you take it for a spin, you imagine driving it to and from business meetings and places of recreation, you take a deep breath and think, "Wow, not many people have this car." You reluctantly return the vehicle and go about your business. The dream car is clear within your vision; However, something's happened. This dream car you thought was only for the select few is suddenly popping up everywhere. This is the law of attraction working its magic. You've focused on your dream car and kept it continually in your mind's eye by the constant viewing of the photo and remembering the memories of your test drive. Now, you've noticed one parked at the local supermarket, while you're out on a run, when you go to collect the kids from school. Was this car always there? Absolutely! Then, why were you not seeing it before? Because you were unaware and had no expectation or thoughts toward it.

What you put in your mind has the ability to reveal a whole new world filled with very tangible opportunities. We're simply walking around blind rather than expectant to what's right in our faces. With this in mind, the law of attraction is all about expecting good and positive things to happen—

for waves of creativity and revolution to flood your mind and life. Many look but few actually see. Sometimes, you have to taste something, touch it, dwell on it and assess it to seriously see it come alive. There are some great opportunities out there in this world, but often the most powerful, life changing and rule breaking opportunities lie within us. Fan this flame of attraction and expectation.

The first time I personally experienced the law of attraction it was because I wanted to surround myself with people who were better than me. I wrote down some key traits I wanted to embrace within my own life and thought about where this type of person might hang out. I used Google, I spoke to a couple of well connected people, and I started to have a clear vision of the type of person with whom I wanted to associate myself. Once I knew what they looked like, it was easier to find them. From there, it was easy to begin expecting my life to become richer, so I can influence, encourage and inspire people to find their deeper calling by introducing them to their inner sniper.

It all starts with creating a mindset that only improves through further self discovery and developing your relationships, mindset and attitude. Welcoming the law of attraction often starts with you being a person of attraction yourself. The hardest person in life to lead is you. If you continually work on you while listening to help others get what they want, you'll always have friends and, more importantly, you'll have qualities that are attractive to others. That's how you build your reputation, influence and business. It's really how you build anything. It's all about relationships: Your ability to serve, share, equip and invest.

I recently attended the funeral of an incredible man. The reason I was so fond of him was his ability to remain consistent and loyal to those he loved despite the challenging conditions he faced within his marriage and his love for local politics. While so many good men and women fall down at the last hurdle, he'd finished this life strong. It's a challenge I set myself to finish this race with strength and distinction. I believe this man finished strong because he knew who he was and surrounded himself with people he loved. He invested in key relationships which gave him delight. And, he was forthright in pursuing and establishing what he loved. There is no greater attraction to anyone than doing what you love, creating a buzz around your endeavours and giving off such a strong sense of purpose and achievement that people applaud you and hold you in high regard.

CHAPTER 21

Influence

Affect the environment in which you are planted.

At the start of writing this book I commissioned myself to write for a minimum of 30 minutes each day, and since that declaration I've fulfilled that promise— only missing a handful of days. I often write in the morning since I've made it the first objective I have each day. My schedule and responsibilities have been increasing significantly over the past few months, and today I was unable to sit down and continue the writing I'd become acquainted to during the morning hours. It's now 2:30pm, and I finally have some time to put toward this book to share what's on my heart. Honestly, I'm not feeling the desire to write and don't know if that's because it's the afternoon or if there are other factors of which I'm unaware. Some may say, "If your'e not in the zone, don't write." To which I say, "Wrong!"

Sometimes you have to do things to get you in the zone. Action is one way we create an environment to encourage the zone, and now I get to be vulnerable and share with you the process of how I'm writing this book. Very few authors, if any, talk about the process of writing a book, but I like to be me and lay it all before you. There is no silver bullet. We've already determined everyone has a story to tell, but how are you going to share yours? I like to be real and honest because it liberates others to do the same. When you push through areas of pain and difficulty, when the last thing you want to do is write but you start writing anyway, you'll start to tap into the zone and words start to flow.

Often starting something is the most difficult fundamental in the whole process. But once you start, you must have key disciplines and motivations to keep moving forward. I made a declaration to write everyday, so I'm forcing myself and actually find myself building momentum even while explaining this very point. Too often we make decisions based on how we feel rather than simply acting and allowing feelings to form or transform by our choice to push through pain and uncertainty. The problem with feelings is they come and they go. You have to decide, regardless of what comes your way (good, bad or ugly), that you have an obligation to yourself and what you want to achieve.

The need to be consistent rather than allowing how you feel in the present state to determine your decisions or actions is a critical one. Sometimes, you've just got to do what you've got to do. When you struggle with taking the easy way out, it's vitally important you don't indulge in negative self talk. For example, I could have quite easily allowed my feelings to override my goal to write today, but I refused. I told my fingers and my brain we're writing today whether they liked it or not. When we see someone talking to themselves, we often label them as crazy. Well, maybe I am a little, but I talk to myself. I speak to my soul and my spirit. I speak blessings and encouragement, which often results in calling myself into action and focusing on the matter in hand— sometimes myself even talks back!

Negative self talk is stunting your growth and future success and needs to be eradicated from your mind and life. When you converse with yourself and speak negatively it produces a victim mindset, one that is helpless and feeling sorry for itself. When you do that, you're closing your eyes and inducing your brain into a coma. You need to know who you are and where you're going. As I've mentioned previously, I encourage myself to "Just do it." If you've scheduled to do something, you better do it because your reputation and success requires it of you.

I want everyone to feel uplifted, educated and motivated— to be all they desire. So many people are out for themselves. While I am extremely driven and focused, I don't prescribe to walking on or over someone to get where I want to go. It's important you succeed with integrity and honour. What is influence? The power to affect the environment you're in, to bring a paradigm shift within your own mind that can ripple and change the culture and thoughts of others. Influence enables you to have an open door into someone's life and mind. You can persuade and alter their view point, but it must be for their benefit and not just yours. On the flip side you know the true character of a man or woman when you give them power. Influence and power put in the hands of the wrong person can be deceiving and manipulative. Adolf Hitler was a man of huge influence and power, but he didn't choose to use this great responsibility to bring freedom and liberty to the human race but instead bondage, pain and death.

Influence enables you to change an attitude, perception or behaviour. I have noticed a few actions and behaviours I practice each day that have increased my influence. I think it's important to note, if you don't develop a character and mindset of servanthood, encouraging and seeing those around you succeed as much as you, having influence can be harmful for you and those around you. I trust if you're reading this book, you're a person of character and want to develop beyond your current skill and value. One law I practice is the law of reciprocation. I respond to it in others as well as genuinely serving those around me. The law of reciprocation can be extremely effective but needs to be harnessed with integrity as it could be used to manipulate a situation or person. When I use the law of reciprocation, it's used to create a win-win.

The whole premise of this law is very simple. I'm sold on helping you get what you want in life. In return, you naturally feel compelled to return the favor. One of the keys of the kingdom is helping someone else succeed. If I take you out for dinner and pay the bill, you'll more than likely take me out for dinner and pay for my bill at a later date. If I invite you to a ball game, you'll more than likely take me out to a ball game. If I buy you a birthday present, when it is my birthday you're more than likely going to buy me a birthday present— unless you have no soul. Look out for opportunities to help people. Who can you encourage or exhort? Who can you recommend or pour your time and energy into?

When I worked in the service industry, I'd constantly look at ways to make a further impression beyond my colleagues that would increase the customer experience, enhance my reputation and increase my tips. I shook the hand of every guest to make a human connection. It was my way of honouring them and thanking them for allowing me to serve them. Customers are not an inconvenience. If you feel your customer is an inconvenience, you're in the wrong job or trade. After the handshake, I'd leave them a couple of mints to leave a lasting impression and give them something of myself. The result was my customers wanting to reciprocate my kindness, and it often resulted in a generous tip or compliment to the managers on shift.

In order for the law of reciprocation to work, it has to cost you something (like your time and attention to detail). If you can master this law, it will be hugely beneficial not just for you, but your whole network and community. It is one of the most powerful laws on this planet. Abuse it, and it may well bite you on the backside. Be wise, and manage it with sincerity and an authentic approach, and it will serve you well.

CHAPTER 22

Change Agent

Disrupting the environment for the greater good.

It's time to become an agent of change and disrupt the current environment and state of affairs. Let's blow a new wind, craft a new culture, instigate a new way of thinking, acting and behaving. If we don't cultivate honour, integrity and leadership we'll be confined to the current constraints of society and our world. Being a change agent starts with you!

If you find yourself fed up, dissatisfied with current conditions, challenges and restrictions, then something inside you may be calling you to go beyond the realms of what's normal and safe and tap into something more. But, what is a change agent exactly? A change agent is laser focused, meticulous, and aware of their inner sniper even with so many voices, distractions and opportunities. They are constantly looking beyond their current circumstances and problems, they take regular time to read and to review their current circumstance and future goals. They are resolute to not take their eye off the target and keep in focus the bigger picture.

Change agents are detailed, they value the process and cherish each step, and they are practical, strategic and systematic. They leave no stone unturned, are extremely resourceful and typically have a large network. Change agents draw people to them like a magnet. They are pioneers and create blueprints and strategies. They often are born leaders who are happy to go first and then share their story to inspire others or create a way where there was no way before. They are energetic fire brands who ignite passion in others. They fan the flame, they make your baby kick, they give you wings to fly, they exude high levels of performance, energy and drive. They are high octane, groundbreaking, earthshaking agents of change who alter and raise up such a fire in their own belly that you can't help but be excited and consumed by their fireball of energy.

Change agents are nomads, they are few and far between. If you come across one and are able to keep them in the wind of your network do so, as these are at a premium and most don't have the luxury of such trail blazers within their network. Watch out for them because they're rising up. They know that carrying the responsibility of being a change agent is much bigger than themselves. They see it as a gift that, in the right hands, will do this world and the people in it good. As with anything, for he or she who is given much, much is required. I immediately think of Frodo Baggins from *Lord of the Rings*. He was a change agent— extremely focused despite the obstacles, the set backs, the demons, the darkness, the overwhelming sense of responsibility and duty to his people. He was faithful. He refused to quit even when blindsided. But, sometimes, he needed help. We all need a Samwise in our lives. Frodo had a path to follow and, when diversion and obstacles came his way, he sought the help of others. He may not have been the most flamboyant, but he stayed positive and encouraged others to believe and persist. We must do the same.

Like Frodo, being a change agent means leaving a legacy and creating a new frontier that has longevity and will encourage others to take up the baton where we left off. Change agents encourage a spirit of belief, conjuring up new expressions of innovation, enterprise and leadership. If it doesn't go beyond yourself, you're simply thinking too small. Frodo's mandate was far bigger than himself. He had a duty to change the environment in which he lived. You also must decide whether to accept a challenge or allow it to pass you by. Being a change agent requires sacrifice and an ability to confront anything in your way, to be resolute and contrite. But, if you accept the responsibility to be a faithful torchbearer and realise it's not about you, you may just lead yourself and others to greatness and a whole new world of exploration and opportunity.

How to Become a Change Agent

- Become meticulously focused, and take time to reflect
- Become detailed and thorough in your strategies
- Be energised, start fires, champion yourself and others
- Create a legacy which is bigger than yourself

CHAPTER 23

Trailblazer

Slam dunk this thing called life.

I hope this book has challenged the way you think and the way you'll live your life going forward. It's been an interesting journey to take time to sit down and write what's within me. Sometimes, the process has been more free-flowing than others, and I've loved the moments of natural flowing content and thoughts that turn into sentences and then chapters. As a rule, a book on personal development is expected to contain around 56,000 words, but I've always liked to break the mould. Why does it have to be 56,000 words? Why can't it be less— or more if you have plenty of inspiration left?

I've deliberated between what is expected, according to experts, and finding further thoughts within me that are both purposeful and instinctive. This whole book is about staying in tune to yourself and creating your own revolution through self discovery— connecting your head with your heart to play out of the core of your passions and strengths. I hope you'll find platforms and stages that bring out the core of your being, with all its skills and emphasis, like a sniper executing with precision and extreme effect.

It seems fitting that this book ends by embodying the whole thought process of embracing your unique self rather than conforming— reinventing and being in harmony with yourself. We can feel huge pressure and expectation from the world, but it's time to be curious and to challenge the status quo. You don't rebel for the sake of being rebellious, you rebel because you seek a different, better way to liberate yourself and others. Stop taking other people's word for it. Be curious, ask questions, and look for new ways to make a difference and provide alternative solutions.

I pride myself on building relationships with key influencers— people like you who read my book, wanting to grow and expand. You must continue to invest in the areas of your life in which you are most influential. Reach out to me via social media, and I will respond personally because I want to connect with a tribe of entrepreneurs who are looking to create a revolution, be audacious and slam dunk this thing called life.

Thank You

My family for their on going love, support and encouragement. Costa Coffee team at Coventry Arena Park. Leif Piano Tea rooms in Royal Leamington Spa. Mr. Aldridge for showing confidence in me as a young man. Joel Rodriguez for loving and honouring me like no other man. Heather Westbrook for her incredible book design and graphics. Meredith Pruden for her editorial prowess and implementation. My personal lord and saviour Jesus Christ whose peace lives within my heart, who rescued my life and gave me the courage to be ME.

#Insidejob is dedicated to my late entrepreneurial grandfather Betrum Ernest Sephton and generous grandmother Kathleen Ellen Spalding.

Made in the USA
San Bernardino, CA
05 March 2016